CONSCIENCE IS MY CROWN

CONSCIENCE IS MY CROWN

A Family's Heroic Witness in an Age of Intolerance

Patricia W. Claus

GRACEWING

First published in England in 2017
by
Gracewing
2 Southern Avenue
Leominster
Herefordshire HR6 0QF
United Kingdom
www.gracewing.co.uk

© 2017 Patricia W. Claus

ISBN 978 085244 880 9

Typeset by Gracewing

Cover design by Bernardita Peña Hurtado,
incorporating a portrait of St Robert Southwell
by an unknown artist

'To be ignorant of what occurred before you were born is to remain perpetually a child. For what is the worth of a human life unless it is woven into the lives of our ancestors by the records of history?'

Marcus Tullius Cicero

'Then came Peter to him, and said, "Lord, how oft shall my brother sin against me, and I forgive him? till seven times?" Jesus saith unto him, "I say not unto thee, Until seven times: but, Until seventy times seven."'

Matthew 18:21

CONTENTS

Illustrations

ACKNOWLEDGEMENTS

HERE ARE MANY people to thank who assisted in the completion of this work: Jeanne Andrews Brunson, my cousin who started it all, Dr Mavis Mate, Professor Emerita, University of Oregon; the Reverend Deiniol Heywood, rector of Great Hampden and Prestwood, Buckinghamshire; David Beames, Oxfordshire Family History Society; Anthony Hadland. From The John Hampden Society; Dr John Adair, Roy Bailey, Derek Lester, Michelle Conway from Oxford University Archives, Bodleian Library. The entire research department at The National Archives at Kew. Special thanks for all the support from Alice and Dr Robert Hawes of the Hampden (Maine) Historical Society.

I thank the Reverend Dr Paul Haffner, of the Gregorian University and Duquesne University, and Editorial Director at Gracewing publishing, for all his constant, unfailing guidance and encouragement during the publishing process, my eternal gratitude. I am grateful to James Claus, for much-needed criticism and for allowing me to complete my family's story. Special acknowledgement is also made to the Oxfordshire History Centre and the Parish of St Peter in Great Haseley, for the sketch of St Peter's church and Great Haseley manor.

I have kept the pre-modern spellings and usages in St Robert Southwell's and Shakespeare's poetry, the wills of the Lenthall family and in all correspondence as I found them in the original sources. In rare cases I have added explanatory words in parentheses as needed, and commas and paragraphs to make the wills readable.

PREFACE

N April of 2012 I received the greatest gift I have ever received in my life, an email from a cousin of mine half a continent away in Houston, Texas. There was no preamble, just an enormous family tree full of English names, starting with my cousin's parents and stretching back to the early 1700s in Hanover, Plymouth County, Massachusetts. From the moment I printed the tree I almost could not let it out of my sight.

Although my family was one in which the importance of history and genealogy were appreciated—I had actually majored in history in college and worked as a curator in a small history museum afterward—I thought my genealogy was as complete as it was ever going to be and I had no burning desire to research any further. My paternal grandfather's line, from Sweden, had been completed in the 1970s by a relative there; my paternal grandmother's line would be hard to trace since her family name on her mother's side had been Anglicized from German and her father was Acadian. I also mistakenly thought that my maternal great-grandparents, working-class Quebec immigrants, would be difficult to research.

But most importantly, despite my family's lifelong love of history and my natural curiosity, I had a true distaste for looking into my maternal grandfather's line since I had always been told that his family disapproved mightily of my French-Canadian, Catholic grandmother—and any bigoted relatives were of zero interest to me. I had always been told that we were 'Scottish on that side'—and that is almost all my grandfather would say about his family. I knew he had

had almost no contact whatsoever with his parents after his marriage in 1925. So these English people coming out of the woodwork were a complete revelation to me.

I took the tree and pored over all the old New England names, names that are the backbone of my beloved native state of Maine, and the Downeast Maine area especially—Thorndike, Jellison, Jordan, and on and on. I knew in my bones at the end of that day that all this information, as wonderful as it was, would only lead me on a quest to go as far back in history as I could. I absolutely had to know the identities of not just some of our ancestors, but all of them, as far as it was humanly possible.

How could I have so callously disregarded my ancestors in the past, I wondered. These were the old-time settlers, the backbone of this New England that I have always loved so very much. Their years of toil and endurance in this unforgiving part of the country deserved better than the complete disregard I had always had for this part of my family, regardless of any estrangement that might have happened almost a century ago.

Mixed with this chagrin was a bit of resentment toward my grandfather. A sweet and gentle man, I knew him until he died when I was eleven, and I am sure whatever he felt for his parents was justified—but it is wrong to deprive future generations of the knowledge of their ancestors, regardless of family arguments, even when dealing with intolerance or bigotry. No human being is without fault, and forgiveness is necessary to move forward in life. I had no idea at that point how much this seemingly never-ending history of conflict between Catholics and Protestants was to figure in the story of my family.

I took the family tree to the Bangor Public Library which has a well-regarded genealogical department. After showing the tree to the librarian there she said she would 'start me off' with three books. I have to admit I wasn't overly impressed, thinking surely there wasn't much likelihood there would be any information about whom, I felt now, were 'my people' in just those three books. As it turned out, after checking the indexes of all three volumes — *The History of Hanover, Massachusetts*; *The History and Records of the First Congregational Church of Hanover, Massachusetts*; and *The History of the Town of Hingham, Massachusetts* — I saw my family everywhere. I devoured the books, and as my knowledge of these ancestors grew so did my shame for having discounted learning about their stories all the years of my life up until then.

Beginning with my immigrant ancestor the Reverend Robert Lenthall, who sailed to Weymouth, Massachusetts in 1638, there was a long line of New England ministers going down almost to the present day — meaning, in a religious colony like Massachusetts, they were well-documented even from the beginning.

The best source of genealogical information by far turned out to be a book referenced in the *History of Hanover*: Frank Farnsworth Starr's *The Eells of Dorchester, Massachusetts,* a huge volume (now digitised) which appears to have been published by another descendant of Robert Lenthall who was a crack amateur genealogist. It contains the most extensive (up to now) retelling of Robert's life anywhere.

A recounting of Robert's experience when he was called before the Massachusetts General Court was combined with information on events which transpired after his return to England, taken from the parish registers of the churches of which he later became the rector, St Mary Magdalene in Great Hampden and St Mary's in Barnes, London (then Surrey).

This information led me to feel I had no option but to try to contact the current rector of St Mary Magdalene to see what he could further tell me of Robert's life, so I emailed the church using the 'A Church Near You' website sponsored by the Church of England. The current rector, the Reverend Deiniol Heywood, kindly sent me an entire page full of information, as well as links to English historical websites which were extremely useful. To my utter delight he added that 'my Robert' may well have been the only person to have ever known the real burial place of 'The Patriot' John Hampden who had been killed in the English Civil Wars.

From the moment I read that sentence I was on a mission to discover all I could about this man who seemed to be at the crux of some extraordinary moments in English and colonial American history. A simple Google search of the Lenthall name led me to a William Lenthall who had been Speaker of the House of Commons from 1640 to 1660. William was a close contemporary of Robert's, born just four years before him in Oxfordshire, not far from the village in Buckinghamshire where Robert had been born, and I felt again in my bones that considering the unusual last name, they must—MUST—be cousins.

An additional mission now was to discern a link between Robert and these political Lenthalls. Using *Burke's Landed Gentry* I found a family tree for the Lenthalls going all the way back to the late 1300s in

Herefordshire. It was a further gift to find that the name wasn't just unusual—a tremendous help when doing genealogy—but unique, originating from an area near the present town of Ludlow, called 'Letehale' in the Domesday book of 1088 (a book that also, to my delight, has been mostly digitised and is available to all) which name later morphed into 'Leinthall Earl' and 'Leinthall Starkes.'

The *Burke's* family tree began with a Roger Lenthall who had been born in the mid-1300s and had two sons, Rowland and Walter. According to the *Burke's* notes on the family, Rowland was a knight who fought with King Henry V at Agincourt in the year 1415. After his return Sir Rowland ransomed many French officers he had captured during the battle, as was the custom of the day. With the proceeds he built onto the original family home at the village then being called Lenthall Starkes, making the edifice quite grand, with crenellations and apparently a fountain. He later was made 'Master of the Robes' to King Henry V as a mark of the esteem in which his monarch had held him since the Agincourt campaign. The Master of the Robes title meant he was in charge of buying the King's clothing and accoutrements and sleeping in the room next to Henry's—an enormous honor and a grave responsibility. Henry gave a painting of himself in his royal finery to the family, and this same painting of Henry V has resided in the home down through the centuries.

From this point onward the family separated into two main branches, as Sir Rowland and his descendants married into the aristocracy for generations while Walter's progeny married into the gentry, but no higher. However, both brothers and their descendants sold the family manor in Herefordshire and moved to

Oxfordshire in the mid-1400s, living for several hundred years thereafter at the manors of Latchford, Great Haseley and Besselsleigh, with my direct ancestors living at Haseley Court and Latchford. It is unknown exactly when the manor was built but the earliest records state that Haseley Court had been granted by William the Conqueror to Milo Crispin and from that time had been home to the Basset family; the Brothertons; the Pipards (from whom the Lenthalls came into the property through marriage); then the many Lenthall generations thereafter.[1]

'Hampton Court in Herefordshire', Hope under Dinmore
The estate was granted by Henry IV to Sir Rowland Lenthall at
the time of his marriage to Margaret Fitzalan, daughter of the
Earl of Arundel and a cousin of the King.

Snowed under by the wealth of information in *Burke's* (although lineage books are known to be notoriously self-promoting and it is always prudent to verify all information in them with primary sources), at this point I thought it would be a good idea to check the records of Oxford University for further clues to Robert's family.

Cambridge and Oxford were the only English universities at that time which granted divinity degrees and Robert would have to have graduated from one of those institutions. Using the wonderfully informative 'Alumni Oxonienses' database, I saw that Oxford's matriculation records stated in 1611 that a Robert Lenthall, 'a clergyman', was bringing his son Robert to study at Oriel College. Not only that, but the matriculation record listed the parishes of which Robert Sr. had had the living. This information was a true gift, real proof of Robert's identity which I could hang my hat on in my mission to link this man to someone — anyone — in the Lenthall clan.

Next I attempted to locate my Robert and his father in this maze of people by contacting the Oxfordshire Family History Society, a link to which was included in the outstanding and comprehensive 'GEN-UKI' gene-alogical database for Great Britain and Ireland. I asked David Beames of the Society for research help and he told me that my last, best hope for doing so was to try searching the enormous database of The National Archives (TNA), based in Kew, England, which con-tains a wealth of legal documents as well as the digitised images of wills of individuals who had owned property in more than one English parish. All of the wills are written in exquisite Old English calligraphy, difficult for the modern reader to make out but very lovely to see, and the wills are beautifully photographed. Upon downloading the documents, one can donate them to the OFHS for transcription into modern English; in exchange the society publishes the documents online for the public to search and use in perpetuity.

By November of 2012 I had downloaded two Lenthall wills which were certainly from the Lenthall clan, but neither mentioned my Robert. This came as a bitter disappointment after having been spoiled by so much success with the family thus far, and I felt I had to let the mission take a rest until after Christmas.

In early January 2013, I downloaded a third will, from another William Lenthall who had died in 1586, and sent it to Dave at the OFHS. I remembered his last emailed words to me when I had told him I was absolutely positive these two families were linked. 'We'll see,' he had said, none too sure this would be the case.

I couldn't wait the several days Dave told me it might take for him to transcribe the will, and I noticed that this third will, more than the first two, was so beautifully and carefully written that it looked like it would be legible to me if I truly applied myself. That evening I took my magnifying glass and went at it.

I could make out almost half of the words of the medieval writing and found myself completely immersed in the lovely calligraphy of this long, complex will. On the fifth page I suddenly was able to make out the words:

> I give to my brother Richard Lenthall such Apparell as appeareth by the schedule hereunto annexed. Also I give to Robert Lenthall his sonne one cowe and ten sheepe or five pounds in money for a stock towards his bringing upp ...

Since I had already determined from the Alumni Oxonienses database that Robert had a son by the same name, who was without a doubt 'my Robert', this was the missing link for which I had been searching for almost an entire year! I was beside myself and my eyes swam with tears as I checked the wording again and again. I couldn't begin to express the gratitude I felt at that moment for all the people at the Archives who had conserved these ancient documents for so many years and then photographed and digitised them so beautifully, making them available to the entire world.

Several other phrases jumped out at me from the will as well—'concealed lands' and 'chantry lands'—and I asked Dave early the next day what these could possibly mean. He referred me to Anthony 'Tony' Hadland, a freelance writer who specializes in English Catholic history, who was kind enough to explain. These 'concealed' and 'chantry' lands were artful terms for confiscated properties resulting from Henry VIII's dissolution of the monasteries beginning in the 1520s. It seems this William Lenthall had bought back some of these lands from the Queen during Elizabeth I's reign and was planning to use the earnings from the land to support the four poorest men of the parish while they prayed for his soul in Purgatory! This was an amazing discovery for me as I had had no inkling whatsoever until then that this was a Catholic family. I was utterly floored by this revelation and felt such a wave of pity as I imagined the hardships these people had endured for generations.

Tony Hadland further confirmed that this was indeed a recusant family by sending me family trees from a book entitled *Blessed Thomas Belson—His Life and Times, 1563-1589* showing how the Lenthalls were part of a large network of intermarried recusant families. One of the families was the Southwells, and a St Robert Southwell was listed as an uncle of the grandson of the William who had written this 1586 will—the same grandson who served at the time of King Charles I and during the Interregnum as the Speaker of the House of Commons—hardly a position a practicing Catholic would have been allowed to hold in that era!

Tony was so intrigued by the language and the nature of the will itself that he asked if I would mind if he wrote an article on it. The document contained many references to God, and some actual texts of prayers which were mixtures of both traditional Catholic prayers and newer ones which were part of the Anglican Book of Common Prayer, something that was extremely unusual for the time to say the least. (Please see the Appendix for a reprint of Tony Hadland's complete article, the text of the William Lenthall will of 1586, and the will of the Reverend Robert Lenthall).

I now realized I had several family mysteries to decipher. First, how could a Catholic recusant family have produced a man who renounced his faith tradition and served a kingdom so completely hostile to that tradition?

Did William and Robert, second cousins as I now knew them to be, know each other? Speaker William Lenthall must have known John Hampden when he was a member of Parliament—and as Robert's cousin, might William have been told of the real resting place of his friend after his death in 1643? And, most fundamentally, how in the world did these men even manage to survive at all during the incredibly turbulent years of the early and mid-seventeenth century? My heart went out to them and I decided that I had to research these men's lives as much as I possibly could—especially the most obscure of the four, the Reverend Robert Lenthall—and combine their lives together in one book so I could compare how they lived through these years, and in a way unite them together forever.

My interest in the religious and political controversies of their time increased when I discovered that one of Robert's great-great grandsons, Robert Lenthal Eells, had married a Mayflower descendant—making me descended from both Pilgrims and English recusants. To be honest I had always been so horrified by Henry VIII's and Elizabeth I's treatment of Catholics and the many years of purges and repression in Britain that I was not exactly an Anglophile. Naturally, like nearly all Americans, I felt a tremendous affection for our mother country and especially as a New Englander, I loved the closeness my region has with England. But from the moment I knew I was related by blood to these people, I began to truly love 'my' new mother country, and my heart began to open up to the realization that perhaps some lessons in real forgiveness were in store for me.

In July of 2013, after beginning to write some notes about the Reverend Robert Lenthall's life, I began to research the life of St Robert Southwell, his relative by marriage. As he was one of the literary martyrs of England (although less well-known than his fellow Jesuit and poet St Edmund Campion) Southwell's life is well-documented. I devoured Fr Christopher Devlin's definitive biography of Robert's life and one day in late July of 2012 I found myself reading that Southwell and William Shakespeare were related by blood, being sixth-generation descendants of Sir Robert Belknap. Not only that, but they were related by marriage as well, as many Catholic families banded together during the years of repression and intermarried with other recusant families across England. This genealogical journey was becoming more fascinating to me with every revelation and I found myself completely overawed, wondering how many more family secrets I was going to be uncovering. But soon I was brought back to earth, as reading the transcript of Southwell's trial was so harrowing and difficult to take emotionally for me that I had to stop and put the book aside for several months.

Meanwhile, through the Reverend Deiniol Heywood's initial letter to me I had become acquainted with the John Hampden Society of Buckinghamshire, a group which commemorates this great son of England who fought and died for the cause of Parliamentarianism and freedom from a state-controlled church. One of the Society's members, Dr John Adair, had written the definitive biography of John Hampden, *A Life of John Hampden the Patriot*, and on my next trip to the Boston Public Library I was able to read his book as well as the Starr volume on the Eells family. Perhaps because there was no mention of a Reverend Lenthall in the Hampden book I felt an even greater sense of being on a mission to fill in the blanks in Robert's life story.

After returning then to the life of Southwell, I came to the conclusion that the main thread of the lives of these interrelated ancestors and relatives was the idea of freedom of religion, which is truly also 'freedom of thought'. So much of what fueled the Great Rebellion, which William Lenthall dealt with for nearly all the years of his Speakership, was this revolutionary concept; it was the same concept for which Robert Lenthall suffered during years of toil and sacrifice, and for

which both Hampden (indirectly) and St Robert Southwell lost their lives.

As I progressed through the writing of the book, I
felt innumerable times as if I was almost through, that
I had crested a wave; but just when I could see land in
the form of an end to the work, another wave of books
I needed to research washed over me. I have said I felt
I was on a mission, with all the haste that phrase
entails; I have tried to tell the stories of these men as
completely as I could while feeling compelled to finish
as quickly as I could because I felt their stories either
had not been told, or, in John Hampden's and St Robert
Southwell's cases, have been sadly largely forgotten
by modern readers and students.

As will be obvious to any reader of this book, all of
these men deserve to have an entire volume devoted
to their life stories. John Hampden and St Robert
Southwell indeed have more than one biography each,
as they should. However, I attempted in this book to
give each man nearly equal consideration regardless
of his station, or notoriety, in life and how much had
previously been written about him; comparatively
little had been written on the Reverend Robert
Lenthall's life, so I used almost every piece of information I could find in the telling of his life story. Sadly I
had to truncate the reams of material written on the
life and exploits of John Hampden, and to a lesser
extent, St Robert Southwell.

William Lenthall's public life was fairly well docu-
mented, and of course as Speaker for all those years,
his public activities were recorded—oftentimes to his
detriment! But in some ways his is the most fascinating
story and personality of all. How many knew at the
time that his family was recusant and that he, in all

likelihood, was acting against his religious conscience as he rose through the ranks of power in an almost completely hostile political world? If he seemed tentative and weak-willed, wasn't that just a way to survive in an increasingly Puritanical society where his family's faith was not respected or valued, and where they were increasingly being marginalized, taxed into pauperhood, and made to feel they were traitors to their own country just by their very existence? In his story I feel we can all see a bit of ourselves, with all our failings and weaknesses as well as perhaps the rare moment of greatness. William was the ultimate survivor. He is so very flawed, sometimes so pitiable, that one can't help loving him.

How I have longed many times to be able to reach back through the generations and help these men through their struggles, to at least assure them that all will eventually be well, that all their efforts to bring England into a modern era of freedom of religion and of thought, and freedom from tyranny, were not in vain.

Although I could never remotely do justice to the lives of these four remarkable ancestors and relatives—or certainly to the entirety of these issues—in one small book, I thought it would be worthwhile to follow the thread of their political and religious struggles through their lifetimes and try to see how I could somehow unite them all in one story, the story of my long-lost and now much-beloved family.

Notes

1   *The Comprehensive Gazetteer of England and Wales*, 1894–1895.

1

'MAY YOU LIVE IN INTERESTING TIMES'

F THIS ANCIENT Chinese taunt is meant to be the ultimate curse, the lives of the Reverend Robert Lenthall, his cousin William Lenthall, John Hampden ('The Patriot'), and Robert Southwell embodied the saying to the fullest, encompassing enough cruel turns of fate to crush men with less fortitude and faith. These four men were linked by bonds of blood and friendship and played fascinating roles in England and the American colonies at a time of almost unimaginable political and religious upheaval.

John Hampden lost his life on the battlefield in 1643 for the causes of Parliamentarianism and freedom from a state-imposed church, having begun his rebellion when he courageously spoke out against the Ship Money tax imposed by King Charles I. Robert Southwell, a Jesuit priest at a time in which being such was illegal, likewise gave his life for his beliefs. His nephew William Lenthall, Speaker of the House of Commons from 1640 to 1660 during the harrowing time leading up to and including the Civil Wars, found himself despised by the people at the end of his career. And his cousin the Reverend Robert Lenthall, after voyaging to the New World, found himself returning to the Old World four years later in 1642 a beaten man—and his trials were only beginning.

The Lenthall family's origins were in Herefordshire, but the family sold their estate, dubbed 'Hampton Court in Herefordshire', in the late 1400s and assumed ownership of the manors of Great Haseley and Latchford in Oxfordshire. During the reign of Henry VIII they held fast to their Catholic heritage. Unlike many families who often had many members on each side of the religious divide, they remained almost entirely Catholic and some duly paid their recusant fines for not attending Church of England services; but all stayed loyal subjects of the monarch. They took care to marry their children into other recusant families whenever possible, like the Southwells, Tempests, Horsemans, Stonors and Belsons.[1]

However, at least once they intermarried with the Hampdens of neighboring Buckinghamshire, who were staunchly Puritan, when Juliana Tempest, a daughter of Anne Lenthall Tempest, married a nephew of John Hampden.[2]

In order to understand the origins of the tremendous religious unrest of Elizabethan times we must remember the reign of Queen Elizabeth I's father Henry VIII and the turmoil he fomented in England in the 1530s. Of Henry's character, Winston Churchill states, in his *History of the English-Speaking Peoples*: 'This enormous man was the nightmare of his advisers. Once a scheme was fixed in his mind ... he always tended to go too far unless restrained. The only secret to managing him ... was to see that dangerous ideas were not permitted to reach him.'[3]

In the year 1529, after twenty years of marriage to his Queen, Catherine, without producing a living son, with Henry becoming increasingly frustrated and desperate every passing year, he came under the spell of Anne Boleyn and was adamant that he must marry her at any price. Henry devised a plan which was predicated on the idea that he and Catherine were in an incestuous relationship due to her previous marriage of twenty weeks to Henry's sickly older brother, Arthur (despite the common belief of those at Court that the marriage was never consummated). Despite his petitions, crafted with the help of theologian Thomas Cranmer, whom Henry later named Archbishop of Canterbury, Henry was unsuccessful in having Pope Clement VIII grant him a divorce.

Cranmer then decided to ask the great English universities for their opinions on the matter, a novel approach to religious decision making which had never been thought of before in the 1500 years of Christianity. Their politic answer, that his marriage to Catherine, Arthur's first wife had indeed been incestuous and therefore unlawful, was used in Parliament to shore up Henry's point of view. Even Sir Thomas More, the brilliant political thinker, visionary humanist and devout family man, later to break so tragically with his sovereign, as Lord Chancellor obediently showed the findings to the House of Commons.

Pope Clement then ordered Henry to abandon Anne within fifteen days or suffer excommunication, and be responsible for imposing the punishment of interdict upon the English people, wherein no one in the entire land could receive the sacraments.

Henry decided he would force members of the Commons to show their loyalty to him by literally standing to one side of the chapel – and those who were against his divorce and annulment scheme, or as he called it, 'the King's prosperity and the prosperity of the Kingdom' — to stand on the other side. As he had correctly judged, a majority stood with him.[4]

Thomas More resigned in protest in 1532 over Henry's attempt at coercion and over his attempt to force him to sign the oath declaring Henry the Supreme Head of the English Church. Henry and Anne together had driven Cardinal Wolsey out of office in 1529 and now with More gone there were even fewer men left to impede Henry's desires. The married Cranmer, newly strengthened in his Lutheran and Calvinist leanings after a trip to the Continent, acquired even more power as Henry's chief adviser when Henry named him Archbishop of Canterbury in 1532 after the Boleyn family campaigned for his appointment. As archbishop, it was widely known that Cranmer, when traveling about the land, had his wife accompany him in a specially-made wooden trunk.[5]

Henry undoubtedly, and justifiably, believed that at this point the Pope had little actual influence on his island, and he was confident he had the political strength within the Kingdom to get his way regarding divorce, remarriage and the crowning of a new queen to give him the sons he craved.

He married Anne and had her crowned by Cranmer on 1 June 1533, thereby cementing forever the break of the English Church with Rome. Although he sent a congratulatory letter to the King, Thomas More did not attend the wedding, a personal snub that the volatile monarch found unforgivable. In 1534 More was asked to appear before a commission and swear the Oath of Supremacy which stated the Crown was the supreme authority in Church matters in England.

More was unsurprisingly charged with treason for not swearing the oath and not supporting Henry's annulment. (In an odd twist of fate, Richard Southwell, grandfather of the poet and martyr Robert Southwell, served as a witness at More's trial. Under oath he would not swear to having heard an incriminating conversation that More was supposed to have had, a conversation that was supposed to have been a pivotal piece of evidence at the trial). The jury nevertheless found More guilty after deliberating for a total of fifteen minutes, and

More was condemned to death.

Sir Thomas More, his father, his household and his descendants by Rowland Lockey, after Hans Holbein the Younger c. 1593.

Henry cemented his own inexorable personal break with Rome when on 6 July 1535, he had Sir Thomas More, the man who was once his beloved friend and loyal servant, beheaded. an act for which the monarch was excommunicated by Pope Clement. More died just as he had stated he was, 'The King's good servant, but God's first', one of Henry's best-known martyrs but only one of untold numbers of men and women who died at his behest.

In Churchill's estimation,

> More stood forth as the defender of all that was finest in the medieval outlook. He represents to history its universality, its belief in spiritual values, and its instinctive sense of other-worldliness. Henry VIII with cruel axe decapitated not only a wise and gifted counselor, but a system which, though it had failed to live up to its ideals in practice, had for long furnished mankind with its brightest dreams.[6]

With More gone, the King, whether he realised it or not at the time, had opened a political Pandora's box.

> Henry (had) realised that the only way to defeat the Pope was to mobilise the political nation and clergy and to empower the former in Parliament to authorise his bid for ecclesiastic supremacy while directing the latter to preach obedience as well as the rectitude of his course … The central problem facing Henry (and all his Tudor and Stuart successors) was how to demobilise the political nation and reforming clergy' once they had served their purpose.[7]

His daughter Elizabeth, then James I, and later Charles I, would struggle with the very same Pandora's box years later as they dealt with an extremely politicised and activist Puritan sect which threatened the existence of the monarchy itself.

'The 'dissolution' of the monasteries, from which the Southwell family was to profit so handsomely, was not a practise that sprang up immediately subsequent to Henry's break with Rome but actually had been used in years prior, on a limited basis, whenever the Crown needed the funds or, in one case, when Cardinal Wolsey desired to finance his donation of Christ Church (later Christ College) to Oxford University.

However, the rise of Thomas Cromwell to the post of Chief adviser to the King meant a systematisation of the practice on an almost industrial scale. Cromwell had been a moneylender but had learned about Machiavellian political manoeuvrings from the best of them all, Cardinal Wolsey. As Churchill states of the dissolution of the monasteries and the redistribution of church land and wealth, 'The main result was in effect, if not intention, to commit the landlord and mercantile classes to the Reformation settlement and the Tudor dynasty.'[8]

Indeed, who would not show appreciation and pledge their loyalty to a monarch who had granted one's family lands in perpetuity? In addition, these wholesale gifts of property changed forever the way land was used throughout England because much of the land became pasturage for sheep. When the landlords realised huge profits from the wool, it only encouraged them to add yet more land for pasturage. This resulted in 'enclosure', the tremendously destructive practise which meant the communal strips of land radiating out from village centers which had been utilised by landless villagers since time immemorial were suddenly appropriated by the local lords, to be combined into huge grazing fields for their own sheep.

For all intents and purposes, the ancient English practises of communal land use were gone forever from the kingdom.

Notes

1   W. Harvey, R. Lee, J. Philpot, W. Ryley, *Visitations of the County of Oxfordshire* (W. H. Turner: London, 1871), p. 200.
2   *Burke's Landed Gentry*, vol. II.
3   W. L. Churchill, *The History of the English-Speaking Peoples, Arranged for One Volume by Henry Steele Commager*, (New York: Dodd, Mead & Co.,1956), p. 125.
4   *Ibid.*, p. 130.
5   *Ibid.*, p. 131.
6   *Ibid.*, p. 132.
7   D. Staloff, *The Making of an American Thinking Class: Intellectuals and Intelligentsia in Puritan Massachusetts*, (Oxford: Oxford University Press, 1998), p. 200.
8   Churchill, *History of the English-Speaking Peoples*, p. 134.

2

THE RISE OF ENGLISH PROTESTANTISM

EW FAMILIES OF the nobility or landed gentry were without some kind of profit from this wholesale usurpation and redistribution of property, including the Lenthalls. Although a staunch Catholic during his lifetime, the William Lenthall who died in 1586 found himself paying Queen Elizabeth to purchase lands which she or her father had appropriated during their reigns—'concealed' lands as it states in his will—lands which would provide an income that could be used for paying 'foure of the poorest men in the parrishe of Haseley' to pray for his soul after his death. These prayers would be said immediately *after* the (Church of England) service was done, 'Uppon Sondayes and ffestivall dayes' and 'kneeling on their knees', according to the will: clearly these were Catholic prayers, to be said for one's soul in Purgatory, a place Protestants had determined did not exist.

One of the prayers to be read includes the verses:

> If Thou O Lord wilt narrowly marke what is done amiss, Oh Lorde who maye abide it. Oh Israell, Trust in the Lorde, for with the Lorde there is mercy, and with him is plenteous redemption. And he shall redeeme Israell from all his sinnes.[1]

So in one of the innumerable ironies of the Catholic/Protestant division in England, a man in Elizabethan times could find himself buying land once stolen from his Church, then using the income from the land to pay men to say prayers for the dead, something only a Catholic would do!

In many ways, in the splintering of England into Protestant and Catholic halves, it seems as if the Catholic part of its history from that point until modern times has taken place on the other side of the looking glass, as if the Kingdom divided into a false, mirror-image life of its own, forcing its subjects to subvert their deepest beliefs for generations.

During this time came the printing of *The Book of Common Prayer* in the English language, the great accomplishment of Thomas Cranmer in the year 1549, an event which perhaps more than any other made the English people come to claim the Bible as their own, and which cemented Henry's personal religious upheaval into one that would encompass the entire nation.

By the time of Mary Tudor's accession to the throne, Protestantism had taken a strong hold throughout the land and her executions of the Protestant bishops Latimer and Ridley did nothing to endear her or her Catholic faith to the nation. Despite her father's many persecutions, including killing almost an entire Carthusian monastery full of monks during the period 1535–1537, it is Mary on whom the term 'Bloody' has hung for centuries.

Beginning with the necessary reforms of how the Catholic Church was run, after these issues were resolved, the Protestant Reformation continued apace in England and on the Continent and morphed into a movement which concerned itself with changing the theology of Christianity itself. In breaking open the strictures and the hierarchy of the Catholic Church, and encouraging all men to decide theological questions for themselves, Protestants in a way opened a Pandora's box; from it would issue innumerable sects, which may or may not have had the entire truth of Christianity. In Churchill's words, 'Protestantism must be saved from its friends.'[2]

Puritanism, the tide that was to take the Reverend Robert Lenthall and thousands of other Englishmen to the New World, arose during Elizabeth I's reign. Although she is known for saying she 'made no windows into mens' souls' she had no patience for this new sect. Elizabeth was justifiably leery of opening her father's Pandora's box further than it had already been cracked, as she knew the Puritans had begun to question her authority in Church matters and they had become known already for their intolerance of those who did not fall in with their views.

In this tense new world Elizabeth undoubtedly believed she had to quash any and all possible unrest. Puritanism and Catholicism were powerful forces which might have done away with each other if it were possible, but both sects agreed that church and state should be separate in England. Elizabeth felt, rightly or wrongly, that she herself and the church she headed would be threatened if either one of them gained power in the land.

And it was also into this world that a man was born who would personify the struggle between Catholicism and the state-imposed church; whose nephew served an institution, Parliament, which exemplified the rise of Puritanism throughout the populace; and whose untimely death would haunt his family for generations to come.

Notes

1   *Will of William Lenthall*, PROB 11/71 (Kew: The National Archives, 1587).
2   W. L. Churchill, *The History of the English-Speaking Peoples, Arranged for One Volume by Henry Steele Commage* (New York: Dodd, Mead & Co., 1956), p. 146.

3

St Robert Southwell

illiam Lenthall's maternal uncle Robert Southwell was born in 1561 at Horsham St Faith's in Norfolk, to Bridget (Copley) and Richard Southwell. The family was mostly recusant despite the fact his grandfather Sir Richard Southwell (who had refused to perjure himself at the trial of St Thomas More) had profited handsomely from the dissolution of the monastery of St Faith's at Horsham. Astoundingly, Sir Richard had in fact been a commissioner for the suppression of the monasteries, and the family manor was built from the stones of the ruined Benedictine priory of St Faith's.

Nevertheless, Sir Richard kept a priest for services in the family manor and brought his children up as faithful Catholics. But this was a time in which there were still 'ex-monks', men who had been turned out of their monasteries through no fault of their own, and roamed the land as paupers; this sad phenomenon had led to the so-called 'Monks' Curse', something which may have come back to haunt the Southwells:

> Of long ago hath been the common voice;
> In evil-gotten goods, the third shall not rejoice.

The later trials of the Southwell family were to figure prominently in a tome entitled *History of Fate and Sacrilege* by Sir Henry Spelman, also of Norfolk. To Spelman, and no doubt to many other recusant Catholics, the Southwells were destined to pay handsomely

for the profits they had made from the dissolution, especially during the lifetimes of the third generation after the desecration of the holy places.[1]
As historian Alice Hogge states,

> Southwell ... was an insider from the start. Indeed, his was a fertile inheritance: the earth, blood and bone of old England—land, rank and wealth—coupled with the canny knack of navigating the new; Robert's grandfather Sir Richard had prospered through four different reigns, no mean achievement, and on his death in 1564 had his family among the richest in England ... Robert's mother's family, the Copleys, was peopled with coming men. It was through the Copleys that Robert Southwell was related to the Cecils and the Bacons, both families now well on the way to becoming dynastic power brokers.[2]

But to what extent these powerful connections would serve to help or hurt Robert was yet to be seen, for his life was not destined to be spent in the halls of influence at Court. From birth a sensitive and studious child, Robert had had a deep spiritual conversion experience in his early teenage years. He left England's shores for the seminary at Douai, France as a fifteen-year-old with the sole intention of returning to his native land to live as an underground priest, saying Mass in secret for recusant Catholics in their homes. He eventually studied at the Roman College (the forerunner of the Gregorian University) in Rome. In 1585, while he was in Rome, Queen Elizabeth passed an act making it illegal for any native-born Englishman to be a priest if he had entered into priests' orders since her accession to the throne in 1558, and she set up an entire network of priest hunters or 'pursuivants'. By the time he finished his studies, Robert undoubtedly had heard that the odds of survival after returning to his homeland as a Catholic clergyman were only one in three.[3]

Just before returning to England Robert, now twenty-five years of age, wrote a letter to his friend John Deckers, a fellow English student. Southwell biographer Christopher Devlin describes the tone of the letter in his *Life of Robert Southwell*:

> He was going through the experience common to brave men on the eve of a great enterprise they have long planned and dreamed of. He was terrified. Southwell wrote '… I know very well that sea and land are gaping wide for me; and lions, as well as wolves, go prowling in search of whom they may devour. But I welcome, more than fear, their fangs. Rather than shrink from them as torturers, I call to them to bring my crown … if I reach, God willing, the lowest rank of happy martyrs, I will not be unmindful of those who have remembered me … Goodbye, as we leave the port, 15th July, 1586.'[4]

Upon arriving at London in 1587 at the completion of his studies, he was forced to endure seeing the barbaric spectacle of human heads placed on pikes atop the Gatehouse at the Tower as he returned by boat to the city. Fr Southwell must have felt he was reliving one of the famous phrases written by his fellow Jesuit and poet, St Edmund Campion, in his 'Bragge', a letter addressed to the Queen's Privy Council. Campion, who had been martyred just five years prior, had written that the Jesuits returned to their native country:

> (E)ither to win you to heaven, or to die upon your pikes … cheerfully to carry the cross you

lay upon us, and never to despair of your
recovery, while we have a man left to enjoy
your Tyburn, or to be racked with your torments, or consumed with your prisons ... I have
no more to say but to recommend your case and
mine to Almightie God, the Searcher of Hearts,
who send us His grace, and set us at accord
before the day of payment, to the end we may
at last be friends in heaven, when all injuries
shall be forgotten.[5]

Robert was able to survive a remarkable six years as a
man on the run, using the surname Cotton and posing
as a well-bred gentleman traveling about the country
until he was needed to say Mass or perform other
sacraments for various families.

Naturally all fugitive priests were compelled to
dress as the society gentlemen they were pretending
to be—meaning in Elizabethan times extremely color-
ful and ornate garb for men. In 1591 a broadside
surfaced in London which was purportedly written by
a turncoat priest who was hoping to expose his fellows
by revealing their identities, appearances and dis-
guises. One of the men, a Henry Bell, was described
as wearing 'a russet fustian doublet with silver lace
and leather hose' and another, a Mr Marten, 'a young
man ... garbed in a plain yellow fustian doublet, his
nether stocks red and his hose the same.'[6]

Accustomed as we are today to seeing priests
wearing the simplest black clothing, it is a jarring
mental image for us to realize these elegantly-dressed
dandies were actually undercover priests, prepared at
any moment to sacrifice their lives. At one point Robert
even learned the sport of falconry so he could play the
part amongst the sporting country gentlemen!

Portrait of St Robert Southwell by an unknown artist.

Scholar Michael Wood relates a story in his 2003 volume *Shakespeare* which paints another vivid portrait of the life of a hunted priest. At one point Robert lived at the London home of Henry Wriothesley, the Earl of Southampton, Shakespeare's patron and a well-known Catholic. As Wood says, 'Elizabeth's Public Enemy Number One had walked the streets in broad daylight in a black velvet cloak, a saintly Scarlet Pimpernel'.[7]

Added to this mysterious and thrilling scene is the implication that Southwell and Shakespeare may easily have met at Southampton House in London, and indeed Southwell may even have said Mass for both men there, since Southwell was the Earl's confessor, a fact which surfaced later as a result of Queen Elizabeth's chief torturer Richard Topcliffe's inquisitions of other recusants.

In late 1587 Robert was invited to live as a house chaplain and confessor at the manor of Anne Howard, the Countess of Arundel and Surrey, whose husband Philip, a former Court favorite, was languishing in the Tower for the crime of returning to the old religion in 1584 and trying to escape England, attempting to sail from Littlehampton.[8]

Despite being one of England's foremost aristocratic families, the Howards were as much prey to the machinations of the Court as any other family. Philip's father Thomas, the Duke of Norfolk, was executed in 1572 for his alleged participation in the Ridolphi Plot in which Mary, Queen of Scots was to replace Elizabeth on the throne of England. Philip, whom even after the death of his father remained for a time one of Elizabeth's favorites, suddenly displeased the Queen when he urged her to marry a French suitor, and he tried to leave the country. He was discovered and arrested; in Elizabeth's view, his attempted escape added to the ignominy of converting to Catholicism. He would never see his home again, dying in the Tower ten years later—but his path would cross with Robert's before too long.

Incredibly, Southwell survived in a tiny, remote room in one wing of the Howard manor on the London Strand and acted as the Countess' confessor for two years, despite her having as a neighbor on one side the Earl of Leicester, Howard's archenemy at Court, and on the other side, the Queen herself when she was resident at Somerset House![9]

Robert applied much of his time in confinement in writing to Earl Philip, instructing him and encouraging him in the faith. The letters became a treatise entitled *The Epistle of Comfort to the Reverend Priests, and to the Honourable, Worshipful, and other of the Lay sort, restrained in durance for the Catholic Faith.* A grand work which attempted to give solace to his coreligionists in this repressive era, it contained as its core message the Christian concept of redemptive suffering—the idea that, according to St Paul, suffering Christians may participate in the salvific nature of Christ himself through their persecution.

As stated in one of St Paul's letters 'Now I (Paul) rejoice in my sufferings for your sake, and in my flesh I complete what is lacking in Christ's afflictions for the sake of his body, that is, the church.' (Col 1:24) Acknowledging the constant trials of life, Southwell wrote 'Our infancy is but a dream, our youth but a madness, our manhood a combat, our age but a sickness, our life misery, our death horror'; yet these never-ending tribulations were but manifestations of 'the livery and cognizance of Christ ... a royal garment'[10] which any Christian should be honored to wear.

After years of being hunted like an animal, Robert was now in even less doubt than he had been on his return to England that he, as one in a long line of Jesuit priests whose heads adorned Traitor's Gate, would become yet another 'victim soul' whose life, like St Paul's, would be poured out for Christ.

The *Epistle* was handed around in secret to Catholics throughout the country, a people who had been entirely deprived of Catholic thought and instruction for years. In the words of Southwell's biographer Christopher Devlin:

> There had been no native literature since the printing presses of Campion and (Robert) Persons had been hunted down; but the stir they had caused throughout England was still vividly remembered. Was not this the time, now when all seemed lost, for a similar gesture?[11]

Since the year 1524 there had been restrictions on the English press, including any and all books allowed to be printed throughout the realm. Originally a response to the Protestant William Tyndale's translation of the Bible which had been printed on the continent, the legislation had been meant as a way to enforce orthodox Catholicism under Henry VIII. As the regime changed, there was no need to change the law—just to reinterpret it according to the new state church.

Under Queen Elizabeth's rule the Stationer's Company in London was now granted a complete monopoly on printing in England. Their charter read in part:

> no manner of person shall print any manner of book or paper of what sort, nature, or in what language soever it may be, except the same be first licensed by Her Majesty ... or by six of her

Privy Council or be perused and licensed by the Archbishops of Canterbury and York, the Bishop of London (and) the Chancellors of both Universities.[12]

Despite the all-encompassing prohibition of the Stationers' Company monopoly, naturally throughout the years many thousands of volumes had been smuggled into England from the Continent, and this situation had not changed in the late sixteenth century.

*Anne Dacre Howard, Countess of Arundel
by John Record, after Wenceslaus Hollar,
after Lucas Vorsterman, published by John Thane.*

Edmund Campion's Jesuit companion Fr Robert Persons, several years Robert's senior, had been the first to set up a Catholic press during Elizabeth's reign in the year 1580. The banned books were then distributed to priests throughout England — but at the same time were slipped into the homes of Protestants without their knowledge, so that the mere possession of the books would not be as much of a red flag to the authorities. The press was moved several times over the years and eventually made its way to the manor of the Stonor family, who lived near Henley in Oxfordshire, where a pamphlet authored by Edmund Campion was printed which tragically led to his capture. The pamphlet, containing ten points of dispute against the Anglican church, was specifically written for Oxford University students and hundreds of copies were distributed to them before commencement ceremonies on the twenty-seventh of October, 1581.[13] It was only a few weeks before the pursuivants caught up with the culprits, and after being taken to the Tower and being racked several times, Campion was martyred on the first of December. Persons fled to France and never returned to England; for the ensuing several years there was no Catholic literature whatsoever printed in the realm.[14]

Due solely to the generosity (and courage) of the Howard family, the printing of Catholic literature was now about to flourish once again in England. Southwell's *Epistle of Comfort* and other works written at the Howard home were distributed in handwritten form, and were now professionally printed and published, mainly due to the benefices of Countess Anne, who had made available to Robert a small house in Acton which served as a place for a clandestine printing press (as well as a secret meeting place for priests).[15]

The Epistle of Comfort was most likely published from this press in 1587.[16] After several years, Robert was finally forced to leave Countess Anne's home in 1589 due to the near-continual harassment of her and the appropriation of her home by the Crown. But the printing press stayed secure in its house in Acton, undiscovered.

Notes

1   C. Devlin, *Life of Robert Southwell* (New York: Farrar, Straus and Cudahy, 1956), pp. 6, 8.

2   A. Hogge, *God's Secret Agents: Queen Elizabeth's Forbidden Priests and the Hatching of the Gunpowder Plot* (New York: Harper Perennial, 2005), pp. 167–168.

3   Devlin, *Life of Robert Southwell*, p. 100.

4   *Ibid.*, pp. 99–100.

5   E. Campion, *Campion's Bragge* (London, 1580), p. 2.

6   Devlin, *Life of Robert Southwell*, p. 230.

7   Hogge, *God's Secret Agents*, p. 165.

8   J. Pearce, *The Quest for Shakespeare* (San Francisco: Ignatius Press, 2008), p. 110.

9   *Ibid.*, p. 132.

10   Hogge, *God's Secret Agents*, p. 166.

11   Pearce, *The Quest for Shakespeare*, p. 137.

12   Hogge, *God's Secret Agents*, p. 161.

13   See St Edmund Campion, *Ten reasons proposed to his adversaries for disputation in the name of the faith and presented to the illustrious members of our universities* (London: Manresa Press, 1914).

14   Hogge, *God's Secret Agents*, pp. 162–163.

15   Devlin, *Life of Robert Southwell*, p. 144.

16   J. Klause, *Shakespeare, the Earl and the Jesuit* (Madison, WI: Dickinson University Press, 2008), p. 41.

4

Content and Rich

FTER THIS RELATIVELY peaceful interlude in his sojournings, Fr Southwell lived as he could, traveling from home to home, and when threatened by the priest hunters, he either ducked into the priest holes located in the homes or hid in small attic rooms until the threat cleared. Living 'in the world but not of the world', Southwell never stopped writing, and in these years he managed to publish several more works, most likely still using the printing press afforded him at the Acton house. Astoundingly, despite the rampant anti-Catholic sentiment of the Crown and society as a whole, the English populace could not get enough of Southwell's works and they were widely read even immediately after his death although it was clear to many exactly who the author was.

In the ensuing years he also wrote the poems *Times Go By Turns* and *Content and Rich* (like almost all his more than seventy poems, published posthumously) both containing the keys to Southwell's character—his ability to be happy and completely at peace in his all-encompassing faith in God, which led to complete indifference to the punishments he knew someday would befall him on earth:

Times Go by Turns

The loppèd tree in time may grow again;
Most naked plants renew both fruit and flower;
The sorest wight may find relief of pain,

The driest soil suck in some moistening shower;
Times go by turns and chances change by course,
From foul to fair, from better hap to worse.
The sea of Fortune doth not ever flow,
She draws her favors to the lowest ebb;
Her time hath equal times to come and go,
Her loom doth weave the fine and coarsest web;
No joy so great but runneth to an end,
No hap so hard but may in fine amend.
Not always a fall of leaf nor ever spring,
No endless night yet not eternal day;
The saddest birds a season find to sing,
The roughest storm a calm may soon allay;
Thus with succeeding turns God tempereth all,
That man may hope to rise yet fear to fall.
A chance may win that by mischance was lost;
The well that holds no great, takes little fish;
In some things all, in all things none are crossed,
Few all they need, but none have all they wish;
Unmeddled joys here to no man befall,
Who least hath some, who most hath never all.[1]

Content and Rich

I dwell in Grace's court
Enrich'd with Virtue's rights;
Faith guides my wit, Love leads my will
Hope all my mind delight;
In lowly vales I mount
To pleasure's highest pitch;
My silly shroud true honor brings,
My poor estate to rich
My conscience is my crown,
Contented thoughts my rest;
My heart is happy in itself,
My bliss is in my breast ...
My wishes are but few,
All easy to fulfill,

I make the limits of my power
The bounds unto my will.
… I feel no care of coin,
Well-doing is my wealth;
My mind to me an empire is,
While grace affordeth health.
I clip high-climbing thoughts,
The wings of swelling pride;
Their fall is worst, that fall from the height,
Of greatest honors slide.
 Sith sails of largest size
The storm doth soonest tear,
I bear so low and small a sail
As freest me from fear.
I wrestle not with rage,
While fury's flame doth burn;
It is in vain to stop the streams
Until the tide doth turn
But when the flame is out,
And ebbing wrath doth end,
I turn a late enlarged foe
Into a quiet friend.[2]

Southwell wrote many longer poems as well, including *St Peter's Complaint*, published posthumously in 1595. In the *Complaint* he harkens back to the rhapsodic language of the Bible's *Song of Solomon* as he describes the eyes of Jesus in terms of the utmost reverence:

Sweet volumes stored with learning fit for saints
Where blissful quires imparadise their minds,
Wherein eternal study never faints,
Still finding all, yet seeking all it finds;
How endless is your labyrinth of bliss,
Where to be lost the sweetest finding is …[3]

In the poem *New Heaven, New War* (which was used by the twentieth-century composer Benjamin Britten in the libretto to his *A Ceremony of Carols*) Southwell describes the innocence and vulnerability of the newborn Jesus and contrasts that with the power He came to represent in the world. The dissonance between these two realities was doubtless mirrored in the times in which Southwell lived, as the innocent Catholics in England were seemingly equally power-less against the might of a state which was determined to crush them. I believe Britten was also mirroring the contradiction of Elizabethan times when he set the poem to similarly dissonant music, as he wrote the choral work in 1942 on a ship in the mid-Atlantic, heading east toward Britain in the middle of a war against ultimate evil. But like the Elizabethan Catho-lics, the free peoples of Europe had the strength of Christ to sustain them:

> …This little babe so few days old,
> Has come to rifle Satan's fold;
> All Hell doth at His presence quake,
> Though He Himself for cold do shake
> For in this weak unarmèd wise
> The gates of hell He will surprise.
> With tears he fights and wins the field,
> His naked breast stands for a shield,
> His battering shot are babyish cries,
> His arrows, looks of weeping eyes,
> His martial ensigns, cold and need,
> And feeble flesh His warrior's steed.
> His camp is pitchèd in a stall,
> His bulwark but a broken wall,
> His crib His trench, hay-stalks His stakes,
> Of shepherds He His muster makes;
> And thus, as sure His foe to wound,
> The angels' trumps alarum sound …[4]

In a more forthright vein Southwell wrote a long prose work titled *Mary Magdalene's Funeral Tears*, published anonymously in 1591. Originally titled *From the Author, R. S., to his Good Cosen, W. S.*, the preface to this long prose meditation[5] became immediately controversial because in it Southwell upbraids poets in general, and one poet in particular who was understood to be William Shakespeare, a distant relative, for writing superficial love poetry at a time of extreme religious persecution and political upheaval. (Both sixth-generation descendants of Sir Robert Belknap, Southwell and Shakespeare belonged to a loosely-knit network of intermarried recusant families).[6]

In printings prior to 1616, the initials of the men had been omitted. Included for the first time in the 1616 St Omer version, the attribution may have been left out previously because it would have been considered dangerous for Southwell to be 'outing' Shakespeare as a Catholic relative of his. Upon the Bard's death in that year, it was then 'safe' for Shakespeare to be named by his distant cousin. At the time of Southwell's writing of the Preface in 1591, Shakespeare had just written *Venus and Adonis* and the poem may have been read by Southwell in manuscript form although it would not be published until 1593.[7]

Recognising his duty as a priest to admonish his flock when they had missed the mark, and not being one to mince words in any case, a passage from Southwell's preface reads:

> Poets, by abusing their talents, and making the follies and feignings of love the customary subject of their base endeavors, have so discredited this faculty, that a poet, a lover, and a liar,

are by many reckoned but three words of one signification.

He continues,

> … the devil so hath he among the rest possessed also most Poets with his idle fancies. For in lieu of solemn and devout matters, to which in duty they owe their abilities, they now busy themselves in expressing such passions as serve only for testimonies to what unworthy affections they have wedded their wills. And because, the best course to let them see the error of their works is to weave a new web in their own loom, I have here laid a few coarse threads together to invite some skillfuller wits to go forward in the same, or to begin some finer piece, wherein may be seen how well verse and virtue suit together.

Southwell ends the preface by saying he hoped Shakespeare (and others) would use his words and add their own 'tunes, and let them, I pray you, be still a part in all your music'.[8]

Although admittedly a stern warning, the open letter to the Bard and other poets was much less dangerous and damning than it would have been if Southwell had declared outright that he knew Shakespeare was Catholic and accused him of misusing his talents at a time of great persecution.

Another, very likely view was that Shakespeare, with a father and daughter who were fine-paying recusant Catholics, was acknowledged by the Queen to also be one of their number. According to scholar Joseph Pearce, Shakespeare, unlike his 'notorious and charismatic' cousin Southwell,

> was not so much a 'secret Catholic' whose faith was unknown to all but a chosen (Catholic) few,

> but that he was considered a 'safe' or 'tame'
> Catholic whose faith was known but was not
> considered a threat to the Queen or the state.[9]

Other scholars through the years have not seen the myriad allusions to Catholic life and worship in Shakespeare's works. Peter Ackroyd states in his biography 'The safest and most likely conclusion must be that despite his manifold Catholic connections Shakespeare professed no particular faith. The church bells did not summon him to worship. They reminded him of decay and time past. Just as he was a man without opinions, so he was a man without beliefs. He subdued his nature to whatever in the drama confronted him. He was, in that sense, above faith.'[10] As Pearce observes, the entire notion of any 'man without opinions' or a 'man without beliefs' beggars belief. No one on earth who has attained the age of sentience can be without opinions or beliefs on possibly hundreds or thousands of subjects, and positing that theory is silly at best. 'Agnosticism is a belief, atheism is a belief, nihilism is a belief; and these beliefs obviously inform our opinions. Shakespeare may or may not have been a believing Catholic, but he clearly could not have been "without beliefs". Such men do not exist.'[11]

Additionally one can view the comment 'above faith' as just another example of the rampant anti-religious tone of modern academe and criticism, always willing to project modern nihilistic worldviews on people living four and five centuries ago. Pearce notes the modern philosopher George Santayana also saw what he desired to see when reading the Bard:

> Shakespeare is remarkable among the poets for
> being without a philosophy and without a
> religion … the absence of religion in Shake-

speare was a sign of his good sense … For Shakespeare, in the matter of religion, the choice lay between Christianity and nothing. He chose nothing; he chose to leave his heroes and himself in the presence of life and of death with no other philosophy than that which the profane world can suggest and understand.[12]

Certainly the lack of understanding of the almost innumerable Catholic references and inferences in Shakespeare's works can be partly attributable to the fact that so many Catholic traditions and expressions had been rooted out of the English landscape and mindset through the centuries of the Protestant state-controlled church. For those with an open mind, the world-views of many of his characters are the complete opposite of nihilism and have everything to do with the traditional world-view of the Church.

Interestingly, according to Shakespeare scholar John Klause, Shakespeare's *Venus and Adonis* as published has striking parallels to Southwell's choice of language in the Preface and it may well be that the Bard expresses his sympathy with his Jesuit cousin between the lines in his characterisation of the futility of martyrdom—if one views the poem as a political allegory, with Queen Elizabeth as Venus, William Cecil, Lord Burghley as the boar and the Earl of Southampton as Adonis.[13] Taking this a step further, the scholar Richard Wilson believes *Venus and Adonis* was an allegory which was 'a critique of martyrdom … a parable of its futility in the sadistic terms of a "hard-favored tyrant" and in a state "most deceiving when it seems most just."'[14]

There is no doubt that Shakespeare, according to numerous scholars, was influenced by Southwell's other writings. In *Shakespeare, the Earl and the Jesuit*, Klause cites many words and phrases repeated by Shakespeare in *Venus* which first appeared in Southwell's *Lewd Love*: 'In the dedication of *Venus and Adonis* to (his patron) Southampton, Shakespeare declares that if his work prove "deformed", he will "never after *eare* so *barren a land, for feare it* yeeld me still so bad a *harvest.*"' Southwell, in 'Lewd Love is Losse', uses much the same language for a different purpose, warning his reader against the empty charms of earthly pleasure:

> Gleane not in *barren soyle* these offal *eares*
> Sith *reap* thou maiest whole *harvestes* of delight.[15]

Regardless of his at times faithless (or, more charitably stated, more subtle and circumspect) relatives and fellow poets, Southwell soldiered on, next writing a response to Queen Elizabeth's 'Proclamation' of November 1591. Although prompted by the Spanish army's landing in France to help fight against the Huguenots, primarily the Proclamation was a screed against Catholics and in particular, Jesuits. It fed on xenophobia and the fear of having yet another Spanish Armada-style invasion of England, this time abetted by the Jesuit order, a theme Elizabeth returned to again and again.

In historian Alice Hogge's review of the *Proclamation* she states that it 'painted the very portrait of treachery. The Catholic missionaries, it explained, were "dissolute young men, criminals, fugitives and rebels, schooled in sedition, pretending to promise Heaven … threatening Damnation" and "Undermining our good Subjects … to train them to their Treasons." This was tabloid language and sentiment, fanning the flames of national paranoia, fuelling the panic, smoking out all those still standing undecided in the midst of England's religious divide. It was effective, low-punching, hard-hitting propaganda — cheap and cheerfully brutal.'[16] Believing this direct assault on his order needed an immediate response, Robert set himself to work. As much as he must have hated to be forced to respond to such defamatory threats from his Queen (actually he inferred that the pursuivant Topcliffe's handwriting was all over the Proclamation) Southwell stated that he dreaded to have 'seemed with our silence to give credit to our obloquies: to which if we do not, it may be imagined that we cannot answer.'[17]

Notes

1   *The Complete Works of Robert Southwell, With Life and Works* (Lexington, KY: Classic Reprint Series, Forgotten Books, 2012), pp. 47–48.

2   *Ibid.*, pp. 57–59.

3   *Ibid.*, p. 23.

4   *Ibid.*, p. 101.

5   J. Klause, *Shakespeare, the Earl and the Jesuit*, (Madison, WI: Dickinson University Press, 2008), p. 44.

6   C. Devlin, *The Life of Robert Southwell*, (New York: Farrar, Straus & Cudahy, 1956), pp. 5, 264.

7   *Ibid.*, p. 261.

8   *The Complete Works of Robert Southwell*, pp. 1–2.

9   J. Pearce, *The Quest for Shakespeare* (San Francisco: Ignatius Press, 2008), p. 119.

10   P. Ackroyd, *Shakespeare: The Biography* (New York: Nan A. Talese/Doubleday, 2005), p. 474.

11   Pearce, *The Quest for Shakespeare*, p. 18–19.

12   *Ibid.*, p. 19.

13   Klause, *Shakespeare, the Earl and the Jesuit*, p. 45.

14   R. Wilson, *A Bloody Question: The Politics of Venus and Adonis*, Article from *Religion and the Arts* (Lancaster University, vol V, issue 3) pp. 297–316.

15 Klause, *Shakespeare, the Earl and the Jesuit*, p. 47. Italics added for emphasis.

16 A. Hogge, *God's Secret Agents: Queen Elizabeth's Secret Priests and the Hatching of the Gunpowder Plot* (New York: Harper Perennial, 2005), p. 159.

17 Devlin, *The Life of Robert Southwell*, p. 245.

5

BEST BELOVED PRINCESS

URING THE WINTER of 1591–92, Garnet, Southwell and several other priests rented a cottage in either Moorfields or Houndsditch (the historical records are unclear which village it was), a place where they could live and write in relative peace and safety, away from the intense pursuivant hunts that had besieged the Catholic community in London since the *Proclamation*. They were living so far 'underground' that they could have fires only at night, not cooking their food during the day for fear someone would see the smoke. Nevertheless, by 10 December 1591 Southwell had finished one of his greatest prose works, addressed to the sovereign herself, a missive distributed in manuscript form only until it was finally published five years after his death, in 1600.[1] Titled *An Humble Supplication to Her Majesty in Answer to the Late Proclamation*, it began with the words 'Most mighty and most merciful, most feared and best beloved Princess …'[2]

Robert started off by wisely imputing that Elizabeth must not have had good counsel; that there was no way any Council worthy of her could possibly have written a directive 'so full farced with contumelious terms'[3] as it was. He went on to warn his best beloved Princess that she was in danger of, in Devlin's words, 'pandering to what was already becoming known as the "mobile vulgus"' (the mob). Southwell believed his great sovereign deserved better than to be advised to use the rabble to destroy the English Jesuits she plainly feared so much. He continued, 'If any displeasing incident fall out, whereof the Authors are either unknown or ashamed, Catholics are made common fathers of such infamous orphans.'[4]

He addressed the infamous Babington Plot, which had occurred six months prior to his re-entering England, and was an early type of sting operation devised to entrap English Catholics in a web of treasonous plans involving the (Catholic) Mary, Queen of Scots acceding to the throne of England. He writes:

> And as for this action of Babington, it was in truth rather a snare to entrap them than any device of their own, since it was both plotted, furthered and finished by Sir Francis Walsingham and his other complies, who laid and hatched all the particulars thereof, as they thought it would best fall out of the discredit of Catholics and cutting off the Queen of Scots.[5]

The secular historian Michael Wood places the story in its true Machiavellian frame:

> The plot perhaps never really existed: the government was by now adept at setting traps to snare unwary and gullible Catholics in order to bring the disaffected out into the open. They used *agents provocateurs*, men rather like Shakespeare's Iago, who pretended to be one thing but were another, and watched as their victims were led to destruction ... Elizabeth asked for a new and even more horrible way to kill the plotters to ensure that they endured the maximum suffering. But she was assured that, applied with skill, hanging, drawing and quartering would satisfy her on that score.[6]

What was happening now in the country he loved so
much was, in his opinion, governance by fear and
scapegoating. As Devlin notes,

> the 'Big Lie' for the apathetic majority, espe-
> cially in the thickly-populated southeast, was
> based on a sure and cynical estimate of their
> lower instincts: their readiness to buy a reputa-
> tion for loyalty at the very easy price of cruelty
> to a defenseless foe … the sting in the tail of the
> Proclamation was the appointment of 'Commis-
> sioners' with absolute power to overhaul the
> households of all 'noblemen, gentlemen, Lords,
> Ladies, Master or Mistress or owner whatso-
> ever' in ferreting out anyone suspected of
> plotting against the Crown or having anything
> to do with Catholic priests, especially Jesuits.[7]

Robert went on to imagine the day of the Last Judgment happening 'in your Majesty's time, a thing not
so impossible as uncertain' when all the past monarchs
of England would rise from their crypts and, as Devlin
says, 'find themselves liable to the same penalties of
felony for the cathedrals they had built and the Masses
they had endowed'.[8]

As historian Hogge relates,

> What reason, he asked, had English Catholics
> to kill the Queen when 'the death of your
> Majesty would be an Alarm to infinite uproars
> and likelier to breed all men a general calamity,
> than Catholics any Cause of Comfort?' If the
> missionaries were rebels and assassins, then
> surely 'we should [have been] trained in Martial
> exercises, busied in politique and Civil affairs,
> hardened to the field, and made to the weapon;
> whereas a thousand eyes and ears are daily
> witnesses that our studies are nothing else but

> Philosophy and Divinity? … what Army soever
> should come against you we will rather yield
> our breasts to be broached by our Country's
> swords, than use our swords to the effusion of
> our Country's blood.'[9]

Perhaps most saliently, Southwell shows Elizabeth that it truly is not from Catholics she had the most to fear; rather, it was the Puritans, from the polar opposite denomination, who were the truly revolutionary force.

> It is a point of the Catholic faith (defended by us
> against the Sectarians of these days) that subjects
> are bound in conscience, under pain of forfeiting
> their right in heaven and incurring the guilt of
> eternal torments, to obey the just laws of their
> Princes; which both the Protestants and Puritans
> deny with their father Mr. Calvin and therefore
> if we were not pressed to that which by the
> general verdict of all ages was judged a breach
> of the law of God, we should never give Your
> Majesty the least cause of displeasure.

But he hastens to add, for fear of being misunderstood to advocate further persecution, that he was 'too well acquainted with the smart of our own punishments to wish any Christian to be partakers of our pains.'[10]

As Hogge relates,

> In light of the extreme penalties still being
> meted out to heretics in Catholic Europe, this
> was a startling concession by the Jesuit. Essen-
> tially, the *Supplication* offered the possibility,
> faint and still barely formed, of a third way, a
> *via media*, in which English Catholics accepted
> the inevitability of their minority status in
> return for an end to their sufferings.[11]

This was perhaps the truest manifestation of South-well's Christian beliefs, an expression of total forgive-ness and mercy considering some Catholics at that time undoubtedly would have liked to replace Eliza-beth on the throne and give back to Protestants the same measure of intolerance which had been meted out to them.

Pearce notes that the ironic fact remains that it was Catholic Englishmen who for the most part fought on the side of their King several decades later during the Rebellion; the (Protestant) Puritans were ultimately those responsible for the monarch's demise.

Notes

1   J. Klause, *Shakespeare, the Earl and the Jesuit* (Madison, WI: Dickinson University Press, 2008), p. 4.

2   C. Devlin, *The Life of Robert Southwell* (New York: Farrar, Straus and Cudahy, 1956), p. 239.

3   *Ibid.*, p. 242.

4   *Ibid.*, p. 243.

5   J. Pearce, *The Quest for Shakespeare* (San Francisco: Ignatius Press, 2008), p. 95.

6   *Ibid.*, p. 95, after M. Wood, *Shakespeare* (New York: Basic Books/Perseus Book Group, 2003), p. 101.

7   Devlin, *The Life of Robert Southwell*, p. 244.

8   *Ibid.*, p. 245.

9   A. Hogge, *God's Secret Agents: Queen Elizabeth's Forbidden Priests and the Hatching of the Gunpowder Plot* (New York: Harper Perennial, 2005), p. 173.

10   Devlin, *The Life of Robert Southwell*, p. 247.

11   Hogge, *God's Secret Agents*, p. 174.

6

'MY MIND TO ME AN EMPIRE IS'

RAGICALLY, AND PREDICTABLY, the *Humble Supplication* made Robert rise to the top of Topcliffe's enemies list; he laid low and his superior, Henry Garnet, dismissed out of hand that there could be any publication of the *Supplication*, although handwritten copies circulated around the country to the usual interested Catholic parties.[1] On 26 June 1592, after six years of living each day just one step ahead of his pursuers, Robert's luck finally came to an end. He was betrayed by Anne Bellamy, a recusant lady who had already lost two brothers to execution, another to torture and exile and a mother who died in prison due to their unwitting assistance to priests who were part of the Babington Plot.

Robert was captured at Uxendon, the Bellamy family manor in Warwickshire, near Harrow. According to historians, Nicholas Jones, one of Topcliffe's pursuivant henchmen and the under-keeper of the Gatehouse, was the man responsible for notifying the waiting Topcliffe that the priest had finally been lured to Uxendon, a trap that had been set for three weeks. To ensure that there be no escape, Anne had even been forced to draw a map of the family manor.[2]

This luckless young lady of an old Warwickshire family had been raped and made pregnant in prison by Sir Richard Topcliffe, Queen Elizabeth's main priest hunter. She was threatened with the further besmirch-ing of her family name unless she gave up Father Robert to Topcliffe. In return for setting up the capture of the priest, she was married off to one of Topcliffe's priest hunters, a Nicholas Jones, and was able to give her child the man's surname.[3] In a sad summation of this twisted tale, Devlin writes:

> And so, well before her child was due, Anne would be married to Nicholas Jones—but married in church with the blessing of her parents, and with the rich manor of Preston from the Bellamy lands as her dowry. In the event, five innocent people, three men and two women, died in great pain, and several others were ruined, in order to provide the weaver's son with a country house.[4]

When he was finally brought face to face with Topcliffe in the hall of Uxendon after being caught in the middle of saying Mass for what was left of the Bellamy family, Garnet reported Topcliffe asking Southwell who he was. According to Hogge,

> Southwell answered, 'A gentleman.' Topcliffe replied, 'No, a priest, a traitor, a Jesuit.' South-well asked Topcliffe to prove this assertion. Topcliffe drew his sword and ran at Southwell. It took a concerted effort to hold the priest-hunter back. All the while, wrote Garnet, South-well watched impassively, seemingly unafraid of what was happening to him.[5]

Southwell blithely responded, 'I see. It is my blood you are after. You may have it as freely as my mother gave it to me.' Topcliffe then sent one of his men, Fitzherbert, to apprise the Queen of the great quarry he had just captured, after having hunted the priest for the entire six years Robert had been back in England. Henry Garnet, who had remained the head of Southwell's Jesuit group since Robert returned home to England and who had contacts at Court, reported that Elizabeth 'heard (the news), I am told, with unwonted merriment.'[6]

In a letter to their former Jesuit professor Claudius Acquaviva, Garnet wrote further of Southwell's odyssey into martyrdom, observing how Robert had been tied up and transported into the city of Westminster. 'Although they passed through the least frequented streets, the report of his capture had spread already through the whole city.'[7] Clearly the underground network of Catholic Londoners were quickly made aware of this poet priest, and without a doubt their horror and grief must have been mixed with awe that he had outwitted Topcliffe for six entire years.

> Queen Elizabeth's chief priest hunter triumphantly wrote the following in a letter to her the next morning: Most Gracious Sovereign ... Having F. Robert Southwell (of my knowledge) the Jesuit in my strong chamber in Westminster... if your Highness' pleasure be to know anything in his heart, to stand against the wall, his feet standing upon the ground and his hands stuck as high as he can reach against the wall, like a trick at Trenchmere (a popular dance of the period), will enforce him to tell all ... the answer of him to the question of the Countess of Arundel, and that of Father Persons deciphereth him. It may please your Majesty to consider that I never did take so weighty of a man ...[8]

We can glean more detail on the type of mistreatment which was in store for Robert by a description of the 'hanging by the hands' torture by a Father Gerard, another English priest of the day, using as the instruments of torture what came to be called 'the manacles'. Fr Gerard describes being hung by his hands from two points on a wall, with his feet just barely being able to touch a stool for support. Periodically the stool would be removed, making the torture more unbearable, and then it would be replaced under Gerard's feet, ensuring the prisoner would not expire or become unconscious, thereby prolonging the ordeal. This method of torture and the concomitant physical processes are thought to be 'the essential pain of crucifixion' by a Dr Hynek, according to biographer Devlin.[9]

Robert was tortured ten separate times by Topcliffe in the 'strong room' in his own home (one of the perks afforded by Her Majesty was the ability of Topcliffe to have his own personal torture chamber constructed to his specifications); he then languished in the Tower and the Gatehouse for the duration of three years. After his removal to the Gatehouse, historian Hogge states, 'the torture stepped up a gear. Now, he was left hanging for even longer periods, his legs bent back and his heels strapped up against his thighs.'[10] Still not one word of information escaped Robert's lips.

According to Robert Cecil, the Earl of Salisbury, (incredibly, a distant cousin of Robert's on his mother's side) and another of Queen Elizabeth's longtime favorites, Southwell showed incredible heroism under torture and never broke:

> Let antiquity boast of of its Roman heroes, and the patience of captives in torments: our own age is not inferior to it, nor do the minds of the English cede to the Romans. There is at present confined one Southwell, a Jesuit, who, thirteen (sic) times most cruelly tortured, cannot be induced to confess anything, not even the color of the horse whereon a certain day he rode, lest

> from some indication his adversaries might
> conjecture in what house, or company of what
> Catholics, he that day was.[11]

If Robert could not be spared from torments by a man who was a blood relative of his and one of the Queen's favorites, at least his strength and endurance under torture was a point of admiration for the gentlemen of the Court. A further compliment came from the Court through Robert's friend and Jesuit brother Garnet, who still had his contacts there. He heard through them that a Councillor was overheard to say, 'No wonder [Catholics] trust these Jesuits with their lives, when, from a man ten times tortured, not one word could be twisted that might lead others into danger.'[12]

In reading of the horrors of these days from the safety of the passage of several centuries, the reader may well wonder why seemingly little or no effort was exerted on the part of Southwell's well-connected family to try to spare him some of these torments, regardless of the danger to the rest of the family. According to Court documents, Robert's father Richard finally petitioned the Queen in July of 1592 on the grounds that

> … if his son had committed anything for which
> by the laws he had deserved death, he might
> suffer death. If not, as he was a gentleman, that
> her Majesty might be pleased to order that he
> should be treated as such, even though he were a
> Jesuit. And that as his father, he might be permit-
> ted to send him what he needed to sustain life.[13]

Surprisingly, Elizabeth acceded to Richard Southwell's request and at some point Robert's tortures ceased. We have no way of knowing exactly when the torture was over or whether Elizabeth ordered it to cease immediately; regardless, at some point it had become clear to everyone that continued physical punishment of this poet priest would prove fruitless. It was known that at the end of July he had been discovered lying

> helpless and neglected in the Gatehouse prison, utterly emaciated, too weak to fend for himself, covered in his own filth, and swarming with maggots. But this state of degradation … now meant nothing to him. In the depth of his consciousness he was aware that the battle was won, the mountain was scaled.[14]

We can imagine the chagrin of Topcliffe, the chief torturer to Her Majesty, upon his complete failure to glean any information whatsoever about the activities of Catholics in England. Devlin says

> Topcliffe was also very conscious, not only that the Queen's eyes were on him, but that the ears of many thousands were straining for the issue of his struggle with this man whose name had been whispered so often in unflattering contrast with his own. 'The Goliath of the Papists' Southwell was considered.[15]

Robert was suddenly transferred to the Tower of London, with his cell in the Lanthorn Tower[16] between the Wakefield and Salt Towers, near Tower Wharf where, compared to what he had endured, the conditions and treatment were relatively civilized. The Countess of Arundel was allowed to give Robert several of his books, the first books he had been able to read for many months, and they were his constant companions in his cell for the three years he was imprisoned at the Tower.

The Tower of London (with Lanthorn Tower)

Although not allowed writing instruments, Robert soon devised a system of writing using a pin to prick words into the margins of the pages in his books. The Countess of Arundel was also able to furnish him with bedding and clothing, perhaps restoring him to a semblance of his former self. Her husband Philip, Earl of Arundel, who was still a prisoner at the Tower himself, was allowed to keep his dog with him and one day, to his complete delight, Robert found Philip's dog coming wagging its tail into his cell. At least he was able to enjoy these small comforts of normal life, and this arrangement lasted until early 1595.[17]

Suddenly, in February of that year, he was thrown by his keepers into 'Limbo', the infamous dungeon of Newgate Prison where prisoners were held so they could be summoned quickly for trial. After surviving Limbo for three or four days, Robert was taken to the King's Bench for trial under Chief Justice Sir John Popham.

Philip Howard, twentieth Earl of Arundel. Engraving by
William Barraud.
Arundel Cathedral in Sussex is dedicated to St Philip Howard,
and a statue of him with his dog is displayed there in
remembrance of the Earl.

Southwell was somehow able to withstand the rigors of his trial despite the fact that he reportedly had trouble breathing correctly due to the severity of his tortures, his voice was weak when he spoke, and the years of torment and imprisonment had taken their toll on his memory. At the outset Attorney General Sir Edward Coke tried to establish Robert's age, in an attempt to prove that according to the statute of 1585, he would be guilty of treason just by dint of being English and a Catholic priest ordained since the beginning of Elizabeth's reign. Devlin writes,

> Seeming to scorn his youth, he asked, 'How old *are* you?' Southwell replied … 'I think I am near the age of our Saviour who lived upon the earth thirty-three years.' Topcliffe then made a great exclamation, saying he 'compared himself to Christ.' 'No, no, cried Southwell, startled and abashed, 'Christ is my Creator and I am a worm created by Him.'[18]

Strikingly, Robert's response has a heart-stopping echo six decades later, in the tragic epitaph of his nephew William Lenthall, 'Vermis sum'. I believe Robert's phrase, like William's epitaph, was taken from one of the Psalms: 'But I am a worm and not a man, scorned by everyone, despised by the people.' (Ps 22:7) It would be difficult to believe Lenthall was not aware of Southwell's remarks at his trial since the transcript was a public record. He clearly desired to link himself with his martyred uncle who had endured so much and then died such a humiliating death.

Upon further questioning, Southwell stated, as an apology for how feeble his memory had become, 'I am decayed in memory with long and close imprisonment, and I have been tortured ten times. I had rather have

endured ten executions.' This disclosure created an
absolute uproar in the courtroom and as Devlin says:

> The entire prosecution was thrown back on the
> defensive. 'I never heard that you were tor-
> tured,' said Chief Justice Sir John Popham. 'I
> never knew that you were racked', said Coke,
> with a new — but illicit — use of the equivocation
> he was about to scarify ... Topcliffe joined in
> with a bellow: 'If he were racked, let me die for
> it!' 'No', shot back Southwell, 'but you have
> another kind of torture, I think, worse than the
> rack.' Robert began to describe his hanging-by-
> the-hands torture for the Court but was inter-
> rupted by Chief Justice Popham. Southwell then
> turned to face the people, the only time he had
> done so during the trial, and stated 'I speak not
> this for myself, but for others, lest they be
> handled so inhumanly as I.' Topcliffe, desperate
> to control the proceedings, then shouted, 'Show
> the marks of your tortures!'

As Devlin continues,

> In the torture chamber, when he had hoped to
> find a poet, he had found a Spartan. But it was
> the poet who turned on him now: 'Ask a
> woman to show her throes!' At that point the
> trial transcript shows Topcliffe beginning to
> ramble and sputter. 'I did but set him against a
> wall ... I had authority to use him as I did ... I
> have the council's letters to show for it ...'
> Southwell replied, 'Thou art a bad man.'[19]

The court, realizing it had lost control of the questioning,
turned then on the issue of 'equivocation', whereby
recusants justified speaking untruthfully to the pursuivants when the lives of priests or others were threatened.
Although Coke likened this practice to perjury,

Southwell maintained it should be likened to what any good subject, indeed Coke himself, would say to someone who was threatening the life of Queen Elizabeth. Would not that good subject lie if asked whether the Queen were in a particular place, in order to save her life? In Devlin's account he states 'The Attorney General remained as one struck by apoplexy'.[20] After some continued questioning by Popham, and jury deliberations lasting a total of fifteen minutes, Robert was found guilty by the jury and was sentenced to be hanged, cut down while alive, then drawn and quartered.

On 19 February 1595 Robert Southwell was brought to Tyburn, near the site of today's Marble Arch. At the last, as he stood on the gibbet before his hanging he was afforded the courtesy of addressing the assembled crowd. After wiping the mud from the tumbrel ride off his face, he turned to the people and addressed them, beginning with a verse from Romans 14:

> Whether we live or whether we die we are the Lord's … For I die because I am a Catholic priest, elected into the Society of Jesus in my youth; nor has any other thing, during the last three years in which I have been imprisoned, been charged against me. This death, therefore, although it may now seem base and ignominious, can to no rightly-thinking person appear doubtful but that it is beyond measure an eternal weight of glory to be wrought in us, who look not to the things which are visible, but to those which are unseen … Into thy hands, Lord, I commend my Spirit.[21]

There was one small hitch, however, in the grisly proceedings. The men who were to remove Robert at the last moment of hanging so that he would still be alive when he was drawn and quartered were suddenly blocked by Charles Blount, later Lord Mountjoy, a Protestant friend of Robert's. In this small act of mercy for his friend, Blount restrained the men until he was sure Robert was no longer suffering and would not still be alive as he was disemboweled, drawn and quartered.[22]

Shakespeare was alone in the pantheon of English writers at the time in that he wrote no elegy, no encomiums upon the death of Elizabeth, a fact noted by all of Elizabethan society. Even more tellingly, in what was perhaps a pointed reference to what he felt to be a lightening of religious oppression after the succession of James I he wrote the comedies *All's Well that Ends Well* and *Measure for Measure*. According to Joseph Pearce, it is clear that a sense of freedom and growing hope infuses both plays. But after the first year of his reign, in which James decreed that recusancy fines would no longer be imposed, the brief dawning of hope which had ensued upon his gaining of the throne led only to a new period of repression after Parliament re-instituted all the old penal laws in 1604.

Pearce notes,

> Many Catholics had held on to their faith grimly in the knowledge that the aging queen could not live forever and in the hope that things would be better under James. Now they were faced with the dark and stark reality that there was to be no respite under the new king. For some, this was the final straw. Realizing that there was no immediate prospect of religious liberty, many succumbed at last to the state religion.[23]

In these dark days of the new repression Shakespeare penned *Othello, Macbeth* and *King Lear*, tragedies which gave vent to some of his darkest political commentaries. In his arguably greatest masterpiece as a playwright, *King Lear*, Shakespeare uses well-known contemporary epithets such as 'God's spies',[24] a contemporary allusion to Jesuits; when reading the play through a Catholic lens it is easy to see the numerous veiled descriptions of the near-hopeless situation in which recusants now found themselves in English society. The only redemption, Shakespeare now seemed to believe, was for the faithful to die for others, just as Jesus had done and Lear is to do in the last scene. One is clearly reminded also of the pendulum-like metaphors in Southwell's *Times Go By Turns*, in which all realities eventually change, all calamities end, and nothing lasts forever, not even death. And appropriately, just like Shakespeare's kinsman and fellow poet, whose martyrdom Shakespeare may have witnessed in 1595, Lear is brave in embracing his fate:

> Come, let's away to prison:
> We two alone will sing like birds i' th' cage:
> When thou dost ask me blessing, I'll kneel down
> And ask of thee forgiveness: so we'll live,
> And pray, and sing, and tell old tales, and laugh
> At gilded butterflies, and hear poor rogues
> Talk of court news; and we'll talk with them too,
> Who loses and who wins, who's in, who's out;
>
> And take upon's the mystery of things,
> As if we were God's spies; and we'll wear out,
> In a walled prison, packs and sects of great ones
> That ebb and flow by th' moon.
> (Act 5, Scene 3; 8–19)
>
> …Upon such sacrifices… the gods themselves throw incense.
> (Act 5, Scene 3; 21–22)

Notes

1   J. Pearce, *The Quest for Shakespeare* (San Francisco: Ignatius Press, 2008), p. 146.
2   A. Hogge, *God's Secret Agents: Queen Elizabeth's Forbidden Priests and the Hatching of the Gunpowder Plot* (New York: Harper Perennial, 2005), p. 176.
3   *Ibid., pp.178–179.*
4   C Devlin, *The Life of Robert Southwell* (New York: Farrar, Straus and Cudahy, 1956), p. 276.
5   Hogge, *God's Secret Agents*, p. 179.
6   Devlin, *The Life of Robert Southwell*, p. 282.
7   Hogge, *God's Secret Agents*, pp. 179–180.
8   Devlin, *Life of Robert Southwell*, p. 284.
9   *Ibid.*, p. 285.
10 Hogge, *God's Secret Agents*, p. 181.
11 *The Complete Works of Robert Southwell, With Life and Works* (Lexington, KY: Classic Reprint Series, Forgotten Books, 2012), p. xviii.
12 Hogge, *God's Secret Agents*, p. 181.
13 *Ibid.*, p. 182.
14 Devlin, *The Life of Robert Southwell*, p. 288.
15 *Ibid.*, p. 284.
16 Hogge, *God's Secret Agents*, p. 182.
17 Devlin, *The Life of Robert Southwell*, p. 295.
18 *Ibid.*, p. 308.
19 *Ibid.*, p. 310.
20 *Ibid.*, p. 313.
21 *The Complete Works of Robert Southwell*, p. xxiii.
22 *Ibid.*, p. xxiv.
23 Pearce, *The Quest for Shakespeare*, p. 149.
24 *Ibid.*, p. 196.

7

THE RISE OF PURITANISM

OBERT LENTHALL SR. was born in 1565 and became perhaps the first Church of England minister in this otherwise strongly recusant family. It is possibly a mark of the family's disapproval of this fact that neither Robert Sr. nor his son are mentioned in the Visitations of Oxfordshire, with Robert's father Richard seemingly the last of his line. His son Robert was born in 1595, the same year as the martyrdom of St Robert Southwell, who was to become his relative by marriage—and there are many other parallels in the lives of these remarkable men. Robert Jr. was not what is termed a 'wet' martyr who died for his faith, like Southwell; but he was assuredly a 'dry' martyr, fated to be strongly censured for his beliefs at a General Court in Massachusetts and later having to flee the colony.

Robert Sr. had secured the living of the Fleetwood family in neighboring Buckinghamshire beginning on 28 June 1604, serving the family as rector of the church of St Peter and St Paul at Great Missenden. By 1611, sixteen-year-old Robert Jr. matriculated at Oriel College, Oxford and in July of 1619 he received his Bachelor of Arts degree from All Soul's College.[1] In 1627 he was given the living of the same church of St Peter and St Paul that his father had had, while on 18 October 1627 Robert the elder transferred to the church at Aston Sandford, near Aylesbury.

It is not known exactly when Robert Jr. became a Puritan in his beliefs. Puritanism was strong in Buckinghamshire and the surrounding counties, so perhaps he was always of a Puritanical bent despite his Church of England position. Churchill says of the growing religious fervor of the time:

> A crack was opening in the surface of English society, a crack which would widen into a gulf … Calvinism, as it spread out over Europe, was a dissolving agency, a violent interruption of historic continuity, and with the return and resurgence of the exiles who had fled from Mary Tudor, an explosive element was lodged in the English church and state which ultimately was to shatter both.[2]

The Puritans, masters of organization that they were, had from the beginning formed their own 'house churches' with their chosen clergy and councils of elders, called presbyters, and they had as an aim the complete separation of church and state, a goal which set them on an immediate collision course with the Crown. They had had several fellow-travellers at Court including Queen Elizabeth's favourite the Earl of Leicester and Francis Walsingham (her 'spymaster') although their ideas were socially revolutionary, aiming for nothing less than changing society's values and its relationship with the state.

Their zealotry fed on the complacent attitude of many Church of England prelates of the day, men who had in their lifetimes seen first the Settlement of Edward VI establishing the state church of the nation; the swing back to Catholicism under Mary; then next, the reinstitution of the English church under Elizabeth. As Churchill states, many ministers tried to keep their heads down and hoped they could just preach 'the religion set forth by her Majesty'—whatever that happened to be—and stay out of trouble.[3]

The lukewarm religious tone of these representatives of the state church did not help the situation when they were faced with the dogmatic energy of the newly-converted Puritans. Moreover, the new 'saints' were expert at disseminating their theological views far and wide in the form of pamphlets, a far cry from many country parsons of the day who, according to Churchill, had 'barely enough Latin to read the old service books, and scarcely were literate enough to deliver a decent sermon.'[4]

As historian Darren Staloff notes, 'The Reformation in England collapsed the religious and political into each other; by eliminating iconic and ritual modes of communication and instruction (by stripping religion of its Catholic traditions), it greatly enhanced the political importance of preaching.'[5] Moreover, beginning in the 1620s Parliament began to publish its opinions on a regular basis, thereby feeding into society's growing appetite for political fodder.

Unsurprisingly, Puritans as a group felt freer as time went on to speculate about not only a possible spiritual homeland within England but an actual new physical homeland, a new Israel they could call their own, one in which their brand of Calvinism would fit and flourish.

Historian Christopher Hill states, in his work *The English Bible*, 'The Bible, then, was the ultimate authority, binding … individuals and households in a bond of loyalty and solidarity above and beyond King and country.'[6] Not surprisingly, a culture of Biblical exegesis grew apace in the gentry and 'the middling sorts' or the proto-middle class of England. Pamphletting, lectures and secret meetings of like-minded souls sprang up in towns and cities and the new modes of apologetics and Puritanical thought found fertile soil in the minds of the great universities at Oxford and Cambridge. The Puritans' worldview did not confine itself to the universities, however, but spread throughout the realm, especially amongst the so-called 'middling sorts' —not the peerage nor the lowest classes but the broad spectrum of English society between those two poles.[7] And it was just this class which came to form the vast flood of those who were to venture across the sea to New England.

However, some historians believe that Puritanism was itself not truly revolutionary at all—rather, it was part of a conservative movement, as Carolingian Calvinists were harkening back to the Puritan-influenced Anglicanism of James I's reign. According to their argument, the real force for revolutionary change would be the Arminian/High Church worldview put forth by Archbishop William Laud beginning in the 1620s. In his quest to restore High Church practices and rituals originating in Catholicism after years of Puritan influence in the Church of England, such as kneeling during prayer, he actually drove many Puritans toward a more extreme, fundamentalist position.[8] Laud even went so far as to favor the reinstitution of the power of Church of England bishops. As Frank Hansford-Miller says of Laud in his life of Hampden, 'He liked law and order and hoped that the Church of England would bring back what he considered to be the traditional heritage of a church—order and ceremonies.'[9] Many 'nonconformist' men at the great universities lost their positions as Laud's purges, aimed not only at Puritans but all other non-Church of England members as well, raged for years during Charles' reign.

Significantly, John Winthrop, later to be the Massachusetts Bay Colony governor for twelve years, was impacted by the Laudian purges when he lost his position in the Court of Wards and Liveries, driving him closer to the decision to emigrate and paving the way for generations of Puritans to populate what would become the Massachusetts Bay Colony.[10]

Fated to be the father of what would come to be called 'The Winthrop Fleet' which brought thousands to the shores of New England, Winthrop was born in 1587 in Groton, Suffolk, to a well-off family of the gentry. As the years progressed it became clear that John had a strong religious interest. He began keeping a journal in 1605 and filled it with musings on his unworthiness and his acknowledgment of himself as a sinner. He acceded to the lordship of the manor of Groton in 1613, the same year he enrolled and began reading the law at Gray's Inn. Undoubtedly expecting to continue in his comfortable life in the law, he took a position at the Court of Wards and Liveries and remained there until 1629 — the year of Charles' dissolution of Parliament. Charles took full advantage of the uproar that followed to purge academe of its nonconformists of every type. In the summer of that year Winthrop saw his life begin to unravel as he lost his coveted position at Court due to Charles' displeasure at his Puritanical ideas.

By the time Winthrop lost his high position he knew instinctively that immigration would now be the only way forward. Later in 1629 he wrote in a letter to a fellow believer

> I am verily persuaded God will bring some
> heavy affliction upon this land, and that speed-
> ily; but be of good comfort ... if the Lord seeth
> it will be good for us, He will provide a shelter
> and a hiding place for us and others ... Evil
> times are coming when the Church must fly into
> the wilderness.[11]

In 1628, most likely without the knowledge of Winthrop, a group of disgruntled Puritans in Dorset had
begun to form a group with the intention of emigrating. Like the previous nonconformists, the Pilgrims
from Scrooby in Nottinghamshire who had originally
fled to Holland in pursuit of religious freedom but who
ended up making the fearsome voyage to North
America, they had lost hope that they would be able
to truly practice their beliefs in the land of their fathers.
A fledgling group headed across the seas in 1628 under
the leadership of John Endecott and settled in the town
of Salem, north of Plymouth.

By the time Winthrop joined forces with the Dorset
group in 1629, becoming their leader in October of that
year, they had received a charter from the King for the
establishment of an entity called 'The Company of the
Massachusetts Bay in New England.' Although the
group was under the strict spiritual leadership of the
Reverend John White, there was a great deal of mercantile interest in founding the new colony, which
served to greatly speed up the venture as it drew
backers who wished to exploit the fisheries and trade
of the New England region.[12]

On 8 April 1630, Winthrop left his homeland and
his wife Margaret (who was just about to give birth)
and sailed with young sons Samuel and Stephen and
several hundred fellow Puritans on the ship *Arbella* for

the shores of the New World. (His grown son Henry sailed separately on the *Talbot* and Margaret was finally able to join John in 1631 with their new baby). On the journey Winthrop delivered a pivotal sermon comparing their pilgrimage to the Biblical story of the Exodus. Truly in these first years of settlement there could be no exaggeration of the epic nature of their voyage, and it was in this sermon that Winthrop first used his phrase 'The City on the Hill' signifying their view that they were in fact establishing a new Jerusalem on the face of the earth. This first small fleet of four ships and several hundred souls, part of the greater 'Winthrop Fleet' totaling eleven ships, settled in what is now Boston, founding one of the great cities of the Americas, the center of religious life and the scene of what was to become the greatest struggle for religious freedom in New England.

In what was to become a defining moment for the colony, and for the eventual self-governance of all the American colonies, once ensconced in their New Jerusalem, their cherished City on a Hill, the group suddenly discovered they could transfer the legal location of the Company to the colony itself rather than operating out of London. It didn't take the leaders long to call the first General Court of the Company in Boston to vote upon its future location. Once that decision was made, it paved the way for a greatly heightened sense of self-determination, much different than the atmosphere of the Plymouth colony several miles to the south, which had struggled for years simply to survive and remained in deep debt to its London creditors, a debt that was never fully repaid.[13]

John Winthrop, through his strong, bordering on aristocratic, leadership style, was instrumental in leading the Company through its first years, acting as governor from 1629 to 1634 and again for several terms in later years, dying in office. In what was to prove a meaningful event for the Reverend Robert Lenthall, the New England system of magistracy was created at this time as well, with a board of eighteen such men to be elected annually by the freemen for the purpose of adjudicating practically all of the relevant business of this religious colony.

After the Mayflower Compact, this was the second attempt in self-governance of a colony three thousand miles away from the motherland, and although imperfect it did give inhabitants a measure of democracy, eventually assuring them they could have two representatives from each town speak for them at the General Court. But this was by no means a utopian dream of religious freedom from the start; Winthrop quickly ruled that only church members could serve as representatives, and after only six years some members felt they had to strike out for what became Connecticut, settling the 'River Towns' in that state and freeing themselves from the strictures of the Bay colony.

As Churchill observes, it was during these times and the ensuing years of settlement of the colonies when England was least able to monitor the major political developments which were rapidly taking place:

> During the critical years of settlement and consolidation in New England the Mother Country was paralyzed by civil war. When the English state again achieved stability it was confronted with self-supporting, self-reliant communities which had evolved traditions and ideas of their own.[14]

What is it ultimately that allowed Puritanism to flourish for the first several decades of American colonial life when the denomination in its home country (though it had many sympathizers throughout society) was never more than a minority sect? According to Staloff, there were three major factors extant in England, and missing in New England, which allowed Puritanism to grow exponentially in America. Perhaps most obviously in the New England colonies there was a complete lack of any ecclesiastical hierarchy to have to fight against. All horizons were open to the ministers to not only exercise their ideas but also to control every aspect of religious expression in the Massachusetts Bay Colony. In addition, New England did not attract the propertyless any more than it did members of the peerage: the lowest classes were more likely to favor the religious status quo of the Church of England and its familiar rituals, while the aristocracy had little interest in theology as a rule.[15]

Moreover, the dominance of Puritanism was complete as, according to Staloff, 'the absence of the peerage made the Puritan divines and godly magistrates the upper class, and the system of cultural domination they imposed made them the ruling class.'[16]

As we have seen, turmoil had been building for decades throughout the entirety of England between Archbishop Laud's Church of England (which in most ways still mirrored the Catholic tradition) and the stripped-down Puritanism which for the most part was fuelling the push to the New England colonies. But according to historians there were particular leanings in Buckinghamshire and the neighboring counties toward Puritanism. Many local members of the gentry had expressed interest in partaking of the American

Puritan experiment, with John Hampden, Viscount
Saye and Sele, Lord Brooke and eight other gentlemen
drafting a patent asking for lands in what is now
Saybrook in the state of Connecticut. There is no proof
the patent was granted by the Earl of Warwick and
The New England Company, and the project may have
been abandoned in 1632.[17]

What is clear is that Lord Saye hoped to emigrate
and must have been at least in the planning stages of
such a voyage. Unfortunately (or fortunately, depend-
ing on one's point of view) he made a condition of his
emigration that the new land called Quonoktacut, 'the
land on the long river', would henceforth be governed,
like England, by an hereditary aristocracy. Fearing for
the stability of a colony governed by ordinary men, be
they magistrates or not, he stated

> 'No wise man would be so foolish as to live
> where every man is master and masters must
> not correct servants: where wise men propose
> and fools deliberate.' His offer was refused by
> the colonists.[18]

No commentary will be offered here about the wisdom
of the representatives in the future legislative bodies of
what came to be the United States — but one can speculate how much power Saye would have come to possess
if he had gotten his wish. More than three thousand
miles from any individual who outranked him, what
could have realistically stopped him or his descendants
if they had made tyrannical decisions, there being no
magistracy as the ultimate legal authority?

The historian David Hume passed on an apocryphal
and quite remarkable story concerning these men apparently being kept from emigrating to the colonies by
order of the King's Privy Council. Hume's story (for

which there is no confirmation elsewhere) states that King Charles, fearful that a group of men including John Hampden, Oliver Cromwell, John Pym, and Sir Arthur Heselrig would foment rebellion in a colony so far from Royal control, issued a proclamation barring the men from leaving. The group, presumably including the men's wives, was already onboard eight ships in the Thames, ready to set sail, 'resolved forever to abandon their native country, and fly to the other extremity of the globe; where they might enjoy lectures and discourses of any length or form which pleased them. The King had afterwards to repent this exercise of his authority.' In his notes Hume states, 'And it is a curious fact, as well with regard to the characters of the men, as of the times. Can any one doubt that the ensuing quarrel was almost entirely theological, not political?'[19]

According to Parliamentary historian Maija Jansson, as dramatic as those events would have been, there is no basis for the story in fact; Hume embroidered it with names of well-known Puritan politicians to dramatise the atmosphere of the country prior to the Civil Wars. There were indeed eight ships about to leave for the Colonies when they were detained, but they were allowed to depart days later and ostensibly made their way across the Atlantic.[20] In addition, John Hampden's wife Elizabeth was pregnant at that time and it is difficult to imagine the couple would risk a transatlantic passage in her condition; and for Hampden to have planned on leaving for the New World without her is almost unthinkable. But Hume's commentary, if not his facts, rings true: what began as Parliament's desire to establish the boundary of where the King's rights ended and where the rights of Parliament began, was quickly devolving into a religious argument.

Notes

1   *Alumni Oxonienses,* 1500–1714, ed. by J. Foster.
2   W. L. Churchill, *The History of the English-Speaking Peoples, Arranged for One Volume by Henry Steele Commager* (New York: Dodd, Mead & Co., 1956), p. 149.
3   *Ibid.,* p. 148.
4   *Ibid.,* p. 148.
5   D. Staloff, *The Making of An American Thinking Class: Intellectuals and Intelligentsia in Puritan Massachusetts* (Oxford: Oxford University Press, 1998), pp. 198–199.
6   C. Hill, *The English Bible and the Seventeenth-Century Revolution* (New York: Penguin, 1993), pp. 6, 72.
7   Staloff, *The Making of An American Thinking Class,* p. 203.
8   P. Collinson, *Elizabethan Political Movements* (Oxford: Clarendon Press, 2004), pp. viii, 60; P. Lake, *Moderate Puritans and the Elizabethan Church* (Cambridge, 1982), p. 57.
9   F. Hansford-Miller, *John Hampden — An Illustrated Life of John Hampden* (Aylesbury: Shire Publications, 1976), p. 9.
10 Staloff, *An American Thinking Class,* p. 5.
11 Churchill, *History of the English-Speaking Peoples,* p. 166.
12 *Ibid.,* p. 167.
13 *Ibid.,* p. 168.
14 *Ibid.,* p. 170.
15 Staloff, *An American Thinking Class,* p. 204.
16 *Ibid.,* p. 204.
17 M. Jansson, *Shared Memory: John Hampden, New World and Old* (Oxford, British Society for Eighteenth-Century Studies, 2008), p. 8.
18 H. R. Williamson, *John Hampden* (London: Hodder and Stoughton, 1939), p. 188.
19 D. Hume, *History of England* (New York: Harper and Brothers, 1868), vol V p. 85.
20 Jansson, *Shared Memory: John Hampden,* p. 6.

8

'THE FREE AIRE OF THE NEW WORLD'

 HUS IT IS hardly surprising that by 1638 the Reverend Robert Jr. had been greatly influenced by the local religious climate. He had by then achieved sufficient notoriety for his Puritan-leaning sympathies that he was invited by the colonists of Weymouth in Massachusetts, many of whom had been his former parishioners, to emigrate and be their pastor. I believe it likely that Lenthall perceived such a need for leadership in the Massachusetts Bay Colony, which had lost many pastors since its inception, that he felt an overwhelming sense of responsibility for former members of his flock there.

Church records indicate that his second daughter Anna ('Nan') had been baptized on 13 August 1637 at Great Missenden. Yet he must have left his comfortable living, and everything else he had ever known in his life on earth, and sailed with wife Susanna and their young family for Weymouth sometime in the winter of 1637/38, an extremely dangerous time of year to cross the Atlantic. For by 10 February 1638, the Reverend Lenthall had not only emigrated but was already being forced to justify his beliefs in front of a conference of ministers in Dorchester, Massachusetts.

Lenthall's former parishioners had met in January 1638 in Weymouth and decided together to sign a blank sheet of paper on which, when he arrived, he was expected to write down a covenant for a new church—his own church. At the time this constituted an unprecedented threat to the way churches in New England were formed, where new congregations were carved out of larger parishes at the behest of local ministers, who decided where and when the new churches would be built, mostly according to the presence or absence of 'the charismatic qualification' of prospective members as a group.[1] In encouraging his followers to create an entirely new church, according to his own written covenant, he was daring to operate outside of the framework of the entire colonial system of governance.

This was an event which caused such extreme alarm in the colony that it was put on the docket to be addressed in February at the Dorchester conference, meant to be a kind of hearing prior to the General Court in March. (As a theocracy in all but name, it was a common occurrence in Massachusetts for Colonial ministers of the Gospel to be called before the General Court composed of the colonial magistrates and assistants. Originally organized as an administrative body, in 1644 the Court became an assembly which grew into the colonial legislative body which is today the state legislature of Massachusetts).

As Archbishop William Laud had tamped down ever stronger on all nonconformists toward the end of the 1630s, the Puritan emigrants to New England had become even more extreme in their fundamentalist views.[2] Their fervor once they found a foothold in the colonies was tempered only upon the outbreak of the truly revolutionary voices of Anne Hutchinson, Samuel Gorton and Roger Williams (and, to a lesser extent, Robert Lenthall) as they attempted to interject their own ideas into the practices of the saints of the 'New England Way'.

Roger Williams in particular was a direct victim of Laud's purges, as he lost his position in the mid-1630s at Cambridge University due to the archbishop, and once in New England Williams lost little time agitating against the magistrates there. Viewing Williams as a rabble rouser, they planned to send him back to England; however he was able to escape and make his way south to Rhode Island. He immediately founded a new colony, and called it Providence—an action both prescient and revolutionary since, in Churchill's words, 'He was the first to put into practice the complete separation of church from lay government, and Rhode Island was the only center in the world at that time where there was complete religious toleration.'[3]

Reacting to these unbridled new lights, the Puritan divines and magistrates in Boston put a quick end to this kind of true radicalism in the rest of New England north of Providence. As Staloff sums up, 'In short, after a radical start, New England quickly returned to its stable early Stuart roots.'[4] In many ways, seen in hindsight, we can appreciate that the magistrates of the Court were somewhat justifiably afraid of the anarchy that could possibly have resulted from unbridled, unregulated forming of religious communities. The population of New England had exploded from three hundred souls in 1629 to fourteen thousand in 1640;[5] the authorities reacted to this pressure by taking whatever measures necessary to preserve the unity of the colony.

Puritan emigrant Samuel Gorton in particular had issues with any kind of governmental authority whatsoever other than that of God and the King of England. What would be viewed today as a near-anarchist, he brooked no interference from the magistrates and divines of the colonies, a view which put him at odds with the entirety of the colonial hierarchy. A staunch believer, no one doubted his subservience to God's will; but he posed such a clear threat to the stability and governance of the colony that not only he but his followers were persecuted for their beliefs — crucially, not their *actions* but their *beliefs* only — which violated any semblance of religious liberty in the colony.

One of Gorton's followers, Francis Weston, who had emigrated to Plymouth in 1632, was sentenced at a 1643 Quarter Court, one of the meetings held four times a year to adjudicate Colony matters, 'to be set on work, & to wear such bolts or irons as may hinder his escape'; he was further enjoined not to 'either by speech or writing, publish, declare, or maintain any of the blasphemous or abominable heresies wherewith he hath been charged by the General Court contained in either of the two books sent unto us.'[6] From all appearances now, Winthrop's cherished and longed-for City on a Hill was beginning to look as if it was going to need a large prison to house all those who differed in opinion from the gospel as seen by the magistrates.

The confluence of the power between the magistrates and the church-based society that was being built in New England was the issue for Gorton; an associated movement, taken to an extreme, was Antinomianism. Much controversy in the theocratic New England colonies of this time sprang from this worldview, in which Christians are considered saved by grace alone, without needing to obey any moral laws at all. (Antinomian means 'opposed to the law.') In its most extreme form, believers thought that as long as they accepted Christ and considered themselves

'sealed by the Spirit' they were for all practical purposes exempt from the practices of morality.[7] Some
who were accused of Antinomian ideas, including
Anne Hutchinson, who was called before the court in
November 1637, further believed they did not even
need ordained ministers to be saved or to live in
communion with God.

Although realizing leadership was needed for any
flock of believers, Robert Lenthall apparently believed
that baptism, and the grace freely given by God,
sufficed for acceptance into church membership (as
opposed to a person publicly relating a private revelation as a prerequisite for membership, which was the
main means of entry into Puritan churches at that
time). As Staloff relates,

> When the recently arrived Thomas Shepard
> asked … how to go about forming a new church
> in 1635, they replied that such as were to join
> should make confession of their faith, and
> declare what work of grace the Lord had
> wrought in them.'[8]

This practice had become the order of the day although
originally, the Bay colony had supported churches by
a tax on all property-holders—but this naturally led to
the property holders believing they were a part of the
church and therefore had a say in running church
business. By the 1630s a system had begun in which
public confessions of faith and proofs of grace were
the only means of entry into many churches. By 1648,
the churches consisted only of the 'visible saints' who
had had such experiences—a system which preserved
the sanctity of the congregations, but which unsurprisingly proved to be an issue of contention for those who
were not included but who were still expected to

support the churches with their taxes.[9] Soon this
untenable situation was rectified by the 'halfway
covenant' which led to the baptizing of a great many
colonists, an action which released a pressure valve
for the colony. But in Lenthall's time, spiritual compromise of that kind in the Colony was years away.[10]

At the February conference, Lenthall testified that

> The covenant of grace and baptism is the inter-
> nal form of a church, and their meeting together
> in God's name to worship God in one place
> gives an outward form of a church. Upon this
> distinction I will lay down my life.[11]

In response to that passionate declaration, a Reverend
Symmes on the panel called Lenthall's bluff and rejoined
sharply, 'Dare you lay down your life upon that?'[12]

There is no direct response recorded from Lenthall
on this salient point, and we have only one paragraph
in his own words in the historical record to give us a
bit of insight. A Captain Keayne was in attendance at
the conference and recorded Lenthall as stating in his
defense: 'I was for witnessing to the Truth, unjustly
cast out of my place, to which I was called by the
people, with whom we sweetly agreed. Now some of
my people came over to N. E. before me, & more I do
expect; & these I take for my people, and hear we
desire to reform ourselves & to go on according to the
Custome of the churches hear (sic).'[13]

In addition to his challenging theological ideas,
Lenthall's unprecedented way of attempting to create
a new church under his own auspices—something
inherently threatening to the entire colonial structure
for many reasons —Lenthall had much to ponder in
the dark New England winter days after the conference. He knew that former Governor John Winthrop,

now a deputy governor of the colony, had been instrumental in the 1637 trial and banishment of the nonconformist Anne Hutchinson and would no doubt continue to wield great power over the court. By the time of the General Court in March, Robert had had a complete reversal of his views. He must have come to the realisation that not only was he not willing to lay down his life for his ideas, he was not even going to be able to strike out on his own theologically, even in this New World.

In Governor Winthrop's *History of New England* he relates of the General Court proceedings:

> The people of this town of Weymouth had invited one Mr Lenthall to come to them, with intention to call him to be their minister. This man, though of good report in England, coming hither, was found to have drunk in some of Mrs Hutchinson's opinions, such as justification of faith, etc., and opposed the gathering of our churches in such a way of mutual stipulation as was practiced among us. From the former he was soon taken off upon conference with Mr Cotton; but he stuck close to to the other, that only baptism was the door of entrance to the church, etc., so as the common sort of people did eagerly embrace his opinions, and some labored to get such church on foot as all baptized ones might communicate in without any further trial of them, etc. ... The magistrates, hearing of this disturbance, thought it needful to stop it betimes ... Mr Lenthall, being convinced both of his own error in judgment, and of his sin in practice to the disturbance of our peace, etc., did openly and freely retract, with expression of much grief of heart for his offence, and did deliver his retraction in writing, under

his hand, in the open court, whereupon he was
enjoined to appear at the next court; and in the
meantime to make and deliver the like recanta-
tion in some public assembly at Weymouth. So
the court stopped any further censure by fine
… though it was much urged by some … One
Mr Britton, who had sided with Mr Lenthall,
was openly *whipped* (author's emphasis)
because he had no estate to answer.[14]

Thomas Lechford, a lawyer who lived in Boston and
observed colonial life from 1638 to 1641 before returning to England, wrote a pamphlet printed in 1642 after
his brief sojourn in the colonies. Known to the colonial
authorities including Thomas Dudley to be a Lenthall
sympathizer, Lechford wrote in his *Plain Dealing, or
Newes from New England*:

A Minister standing upon his ministry, as of the
Church of England, and arguing against their
covenant, and being elected by some of Weymouth to be their Minister, was compelled to
recant some words; one (man) that made the
election, & got hands to the paper, was fined 10
pounds and thereupon saying a few crosse words,
5 pound more, and paid it down presently.[15]

It would be a comic scene were it not so tragic. One
can only imagine the frustration and chagrin felt by
Lenthall only months after bringing his young family,
including a newborn, across the ocean to a new world
full of every kind of hardship—bitterly cold winters,
increasing tensions with the Native Americans, and
the lack of the most basic comforts of life they had
enjoyed in England. After being forced to submit his
will to the whims of the colonial court and to witness
the public humiliation and whipping of a close friend,

this Oxford-educated vicar must have begun to doubt his decision to come to a new world full of intolerance.

In *The Eells Family of Dorchester, Massachusetts 1633–1821*, Frank Farnsworth Starr writes 'It will be remembered that at the Court held in March 1638 Lenthall was appointed to appear at the next court. There is no record of his appearance, and he probably soon left the colony.'[16]

Possibly in a desperate attempt to salvage his reputation (and perhaps his sanity) before having to abandon the colonies altogether, Lenthall pinned his hopes on the fringe of the American experiment in theocracy, the new colony of Rhode Island, settled by Roger Williams (who also founded the first Baptist church in the Americas) and the now-banished Anne Hutchinson. By 6 August 1640, the Reverend Lenthall is shown in the historical record as being a resident of Newport, Rhode Island, where he was elected a Freeman (a registered voter).[17]

In a legal action taken by his future son-in-law Samuel Eells in 1687, we see that Lenthall, as a mark of the esteem in which he was held by the growing community of Newport, was granted 104 acres of land (thereafter called 'Lenthall's Plaine') for the building of a school, with the understanding that he was to be the headmaster.[18] We can imagine today that perhaps, just perhaps, Robert began to hope that his pilgrimage to the New World had not been in vain, and that he was once again appreciated by his peers. If all his years in the ministry had not borne fruit in a new pastoral position, at least his years at Oxford would not have been wasted, as he would be founding an entire educational system for one of the new colonies.

However, this new opportunity did not become a reality for Lenthall, and, for sadly familiar reasons, he had left his teaching position in Newport for his old home in England by the time of the General Court meeting of March, 1642.[19] In *Winthrop's Journal*, John Winthrop, governor of the Massachusetts Bay Colony from 1630 to 1642, relates the story of Robert's final confrontation in the colonies. The controversy centered on the Newport teacher Nicholas Easton, who was, according to Winthrop, 'A man very bold, though ignorant' who held that 'man had no power or will in himself, but as he is acted (on) by God, and seeing that God filled all things, nothing could be or move but by Him ... He must be the author of sin.'

Easton and his followers

> professed to abhor the consequences (of this concept) but still defended the propositions ... not apprehending how God could make a creature as it were in Himself, and yet no part of His essence; the light is in the air, and in every part of it, yet it is not air; but a distinct thing from it ... Their minister, Mr Clark, and Mr Lenthall ... dissented and publicly opposed, whereby it grew to such heat of contention that it made a schism among them.[20]

In the very last Journal entry concerning Robert Lenthall, Winthrop rather snidely noted '(T)his gentleman did not tarry here long. I find him gone to England the next year but one ... It seems the New Lights of Rhode Island were willing to have advantage of the old light.'[21] No further explanation is found in the historical record concerning Robert's final break with the churches of the colonies.

Leaving his two eldest daughters Marianne and Nan in Connecticut with his wife's brother Thomas Laughton,[22] Robert, Susanna and the two youngest children Adrian and Sarah sailed for England, having abandoned their great adventure after four turbulent years. But at least Robert had friends and relatives who welcomed him back to the family fold and the familiar environs of Buckinghamshire. By 1643 Lenthall had received the living of the Hampden family and had returned to the Anglican world, becoming the rector of St Mary Magdalene church in Great Hampden.[23] He had arrived just in time to help his old friend John Hampden and his family in their ultimate time of need.

Notes

1   D. Staloff, *The Making of An American Thinking Class: Intellectuals and Intelligentsia in Puritan Massachusetts* (Oxford: Oxford University Press, 1998), p. 29.

2   S. Foster, *The Long Argument: English Puritanism and the Shaping of New England Culture, 1570–1700* (Williamsburg, Virginia: Omohundro Institute of Early American History and Culture, 1996), pp. 138, 174.

3   W. L. Churchill, *The History of the English-Speaking Peoples, Arranged for One Volume by Henry Steele Commager* (New York: Dodd, Mead & Co., 1956), p. 169.

4   Staloff, *An American Thinking Class*, p. 197.

5   Churchill, *The History of the English-Speaking Peoples*, p. 168.

6   R. C. Anderson, *Pilgrim Migration: Immigrants to Plymouth Colony 1620–1633* (Boston: New England Historic Genealogical Society, 2004), p. 489.

7   Staloff, *An American Thinking Class*, p. 44.

8   *Ibid.*, p. 29.

9   E. S. Morgan, *Visible Saints: The History of a Puritan Idea* (Cornell University Press, 1965), p. 100.

10 J. M. Bumstead, *A Well-Bounded Toleration: Church and State in the Plymouth Colony*, from *A Journal of Church and State*, (Plimoth Plantation, 1968) vol X, No 2, p. 266.

11 Staloff, *An American Thinking Class*, p. 102.

12   *Conference of the Elders of Massachusetts with the Reverend Robert Lenthall, of Weymouth, Held at Dorchester, Feb. 10, 1639*, Congregational Church Quarterly, #19 (1877), p. 238.

13   E. Stiles, *Notes from 1639 Conference* by Captain Robert Keaynes (Boston, 1771).

14   J. Winthrop, *History of New England, Ed. By J. Savage* (Boston: Scribner and Sons, 1908) vol I, p. 346.

15   T. Lechford, *Plain Dealing, or Newes from New England* (Boston: Trumbull edition, 1867), pp. 57–58.

16   F. Farnsworth Starr, *The Eells Family of Dorchester, Massachusetts, 1633–1821* (Middletown, Connecticut, 1903), pp. 184–185.

17   *Rhode Island Colonial Records*, vol I, p. 119.

18   Winthrop, *History of New England,* p. 39.

19   *Rhode Island Colonial Records,* p. 110.

20   Winthrop, *History of New England,* p. 39.

21   *Ibid.,* p. 39

22   Farnsworth-Starr, *The Eells Family,* p. 190.

23   *Parish Register of St Mary Magdalene, Great Hampden, Ed. by E. A. Ebblewhite* (1888), p. 153.

9

GOD OR THE KING

OHN HAMPDEN WAS born in 1595 to William Hampden and his wife Elizabeth Cromwell (the sister of Oliver Cromwell's father Robert) at the family's town home in London. He became heir at the tender age of three to the ancient manor of Hampden House at Great Hampden, Buckinghamshire, the family having held that land since Edward the Confessor granted it to them. John attended Lord Williams' Grammar School at Thame, Oxfordshire, along with William Lenthall, born in 1591, a second cousin and almost exact contemporary of the Reverend Robert Lenthall.[1] It is unknown if Robert also attended the Thame School, but it is likely, considering the ties the family had to the area. As the editor of the Parish Register of St Mary Magdalene, E. B. Ebblewhite, relates, '(Robert) Lenthall was only two years Hampden's junior, and it is not unlikely that he may have been at Thame Grammar School with him. The two families were connected distantly, at least by marriage, but still more closely, perhaps, as friends and neighbors, and by identity in education and politics.'[2] Prior to the most recent research John Hampden was thought to have been born in 1593 but new evidence suggests 1595 as the more probable year.

In the years since attending the Thame School John Hampden had led the well-rounded life of a Bucks country squire's son, having many close friends and a

wide range of interests. Surprisingly, he had no incli-
nation to, or experience whatsoever in, the military but
rather aimed toward a career at the Bar, just like his
friend and classmate William Lenthall.

He became a member of the Inner Temple in 1613 at
the age of twenty and began his Parliamentary career
in 1621 representing Grampound in Cornwall.
Hampden quickly became known for his ease in dealing
with his colleagues. In his monumental work *History of
the Rebellion and Civil Wars of England,* Edward Hyde,
the Earl of Clarendon states of Hampden:

> He was not a man of many words, and rarely
> began the discourse ... but a very weighty
> speaker and, after he had heard a full debate
> and observed how the House was like to be
> inclined, took up the argument and ... craftily
> so stated it that he commonly conducted it to
> the conclusion he desired; and if he found he
> could not do that, he never was without the
> dexterity to divert the debate to another time.[3]

Hyde further observes

> He made so great a show of civility and
> modesty and humility and always of mistrust-
> ing his own judgment and of esteeming his with
> whom he conferred for the present, that he
> seemed to have no opinions or resolutions but
> such as he contracted from the information he
> received upon the discourses of others.[4]

Indeed, this may well have been the left-handed
compliment it seems to be, as Hyde wrote his *History*
in exile after the end of the Civil Wars, trying to limn
the development of these dangerous years of the
growing rebellion. He was honestly in awe of Hampden's smoothness and complete ease in winning others

to his side, but he later viewed how such men could change the course of English history through the lens of the loss of his beloved king. Hyde had been won over to Charles' side in 1642 after initially favoring Parliamentarianism from the time of the Ship Money controversy, and he immediately became the mouthpiece for Charles, authoring, among many other things, the Crown's response to the Remonstrance.

Portrait of John Hampden, by an unknown artist. From the collection of the Earl of St Germans.

In contrast, Hampden's cousin Oliver Cromwell invited a distinctly harsher characterisation of his ability to express himself. Historian Antonia Fraser describes Cromwell's verbal habits thus:

> ...(T)hat extraordinarily rambling and obscure mode of expression which seemed to possess Cromwell like an evil spirit whenever the general issue was most difficult and in doubt. As Protector this tortured language became a distinct feature of his oratory ... he was accused at the time of employing such ambiguities deliberately in order to conceal his sense.

She adds that

> Later Sir Roger l'Estrange believed the 'tangling' of his discourses to be deliberate: 'The skill of his part lay in this—neither to be mistaken by his friends, nor understood by his enemies. By this middle course he gained time to remove obstructions and ripen occasions ...'[5]

The formative issue of Hampden's Parliamentary career reared its head beginning in September of 1626, when in an attempt to fund the Royal Navy, the Privy Council decided on a forced loan scheme. Hampden, believing the monarch could not legally order monies to be paid into what basically would be a royal purse over which Parliament would have no control, refused to pay the tax, along with several peers and MPs.

Perhaps most importantly, it looked to many as if this forced loan would be a convenient way for Charles to be able to avoid ever calling another Parliament again, since all Crown expenditures normally had to be voted on and approved by the body. Not only that, but if the King wished to receive more income from the tax, he could simply raise the assessed values of the properties in question. And once any amount could be raised in this manner, what was to stop Charles from possibly funding a standing militia which could be used to put down insurrections of his own people?

Responding to these grave concerns, Charles took it upon himself to ask for a ruling by a panel of judges headed by a former Speaker of the House, Lord Chief Justice Finch. Charles won by a decision of ten to two[6] and Hampden and several other protestors were thrown into the Gatehouse jail in the City (the place of St Robert Southwell's incarceration thirty-six years earlier), where he was held until January 1628.[7]

The release of Hampden and seventy-five other protestors against the forced loan scheme could seem to intimate that Charles was backing down on the plan; but conversely this may have been done only to soften public opinion to widening the scheme. On 11 February 1628 Charles' Privy Council issued writs for Ship Money not only from the maritime counties but from all shires in the realm, finally making it clear that the scheme took the form of a property tax on all land, not just land in the ports and seaboard counties, which had been the practice since Elizabethan times. Because of the widespread popular opposition to the tax, especially amongst the gentry, the King's ministers withdrew the Ship Money proposal later in 1628.

But this issue remained a volatile one, added to the long-standing fear that the King was being controlled by his Catholic Queen, Henrietta, daughter of the French King Henry IV. This dread mixed with concern over whether or not the King's officers had the right to confiscate 'tonnage and poundage' of goods seized by Customs officers, a fee which technically should have gone to the Customs officers themselves.

A meaningful analysis of the dilemma facing Parliamentarians had been made by Sir John Eliot at the 1628 opening of Parliament. In speaking of the connection Puritans were beginning to make between Ship Money, the tonnage and poundage controversy and the issue of religion he stated

> So, sir, as I said, let us clearly understand the danger we are in and that it proceeds from the habit of disregarding and violating laws; that it is laws which regulate liberty, and the safety of our liberties which secures religion.[8]

As a partial response to these ever-increasing concerns, an act entitled 'The Petition of Right' was passed by Parliament in June of 1628. In it, rules were laid down forbidding the levying of taxes without an Act of Parliament regarding taxation, the enforced housing of soldiers in private homes without reimbursement, and unlawful imprisonment by the King's fiat. This legislation, still in force today, also came to serve as the basis for several amendments to the American Constitution. But Charles soon exploited an easy way to drive a wedge into the force of this new law by stating that Ship Money was needed as a vital contribution toward the defence of the country. In historian Hugh Ross Williamson's view, the Ship Money tax was a non-starter since, according to the mindset of the Parliamentarians,

> if Charles used the money for the privy purse he could rule indefinitely without Parliament. Hampden saw this as clearly as Laud. If, on the other hand, he devoted it to its avowed purpose of equipping an armed force under his command in time of peace, it was even more dangerous. So, however the proceeds were

employed, the success of Ship-Money meant
the failure of freedom.[9]

Another focus of concern regarding the ever-burgeon-
ing Royal power was Charles' new idea that the Star
Chamber, originally set up as a royal court for the
address of legal wrongs, should now be used to decide
constitutional issues as well, rather than Parliament
itself. Since the Star Chamber consisted of the monarch's Privy Council plus two Chief Justices, this new
royal scheme abandoned even a pretence of impartial-
ity. Later in 1628, Charles drew up what became
known as the 'Royal Declaration' as a new preamble
to the historical 'The 39 Articles' act which governed
the Church of England. The act stipulated, among
many other things, that Parliament was barred from
any interference in religion in England; Charles added
assurances that the Act must be interpreted literally,
not subjectively, as it sometimes had been in the past.

If strictly enforced, the Star Chamber measure
combined with the tightening of the interpretation of
the 39 Articles would effectively give Charles carte
blanche to personally direct both the law of the land
and the religion of the realm, the major cruxes of all
dissension in England—for all intents and purposes
amounting to the rule of an absolute monarch. According to Williamson,

> The irreconcilable division was again evident.
> To Eliot and Pym and Hampden, final authority
> resided in the Crown acting with Parliament;
> from them all other courts derived their power.
> To the King and (Archbishop) Laud, final
> authority resided in the Crown alone and
> Parliament was merely one organization, differ-
> ing perhaps in degree but not in kind from the

Star Chamber, the High Commission and the
Judiciary, through which the Royal prerogative
might be put into effect.[10]

King Charles I
National Portrait Gallery

Williamson further described the atmosphere at the
time of this sitting of Parliament: 'None doubted that
the King was God's lieutenant. Never for one moment
had they ascribed to him personally the responsibility
for misgovernment';[11] rather, in the past they had
always had a favorite scapegoat, George Villiers, Duke

of Buckingham and Charles' best friend. With Buckingham now removed from the scene after his assassination, the opposition was beginning to realize it was the King and the King only who truly had been making the unpopular decisions:

> But now Charles had revealed the truth. He had told them, as plainly as if he had spoken the very words: 'Not Buckingham, but the King'. With all the authority of that mystical and divine right which, in England, was his uniquely and alone—a power far transcending any legal definitions of the boundary of the prerogative—he had sanctioned every error and, by his intervention, had made it sacrilege to deny them. The Commons were afraid.[12]

Williamson wrote that the Puritans' evolving progression of thought as events unfolded over these months

> perhaps was not over-difficult for men who, in the dark night of the soul, had wrestled with God for their own salvation. Thus the choice, as they envisaged it, was not between obedience and disobedience to God in the person of the King, but between justice and injustice, between tyranny and liberty. The Royalist in later years would learn to cry: 'For God and the King' but for the Puritan it became all too soon, 'God or the King'.[13]

Very little imagination is needed to see the continuation of this idea in the worldview of the American colonists in the ensuing years.

The confluence of all these issues reached such a critical point in the House that on 2 March 1629 King Charles felt he was compelled to send guards to disperse that sitting of Parliament. As the guards approached the Chapel, Sir John Eliot drew up a motion condemning

> those who made Popish innovations on religion
> on one hand, and against those who advised
> the taking or paying of tonnage or poundage
> illegally: such men should be accounted trai-
> tors, 'capital enemies of the state.'

This was treasonable language, such that the paper on which Eliot wrote the motion was thrown, or allowed to fall, into the fire which warmed the chamber.

To ensure that the body would be able to hear the resolution, Benjamin Valentine and Denzil Holles physically held down the Speaker, Sir John Finch, in his chair while the motion was being read. 'God's wounds! bellowed Holles. You shall sit till we please to rise.'[14] The Speaker refused to allow any speeches and the motion was unsurprisingly passed immediately by a general acclamation of the members.

Eliot's clear and perilous intention upon the sitting of the next Parliament was to proceed against, in his words, 'the person of that man.'[15] Predictably, Charles simply refused to call another Parliament for 11 long years, the years of his 'Personal Rule'. And Eliot, along with eight other members, suddenly found himself imprisoned in the Tower, where he languished for three years; he died on 27 November 1632, impenitent and unyielding to the end. Upon his death, Eliot's eldest son asked Charles if he would release the body so Eliot could be interred in the family crypt. Charles refused and Eliot was buried just outside the Tower.

By the year 1634, Ship Money had been responsible for adding in excess of £100,000 to Charles' coffers;[16] there was incomplete obedience to the payment of the tax, but clearly many saw no problem with the concept or did not wish to stand against the Crown.

However, only four years after Eliot's death, in 1636, the issue came to a head again when Charles issued his third writ for the tax, and Hampden again refused to pay the 20 shillings imposed on his land at Stoke Mandeville. To most today, the power of the state to levy a tax on all its people from inland as well as maritime counties for the maintenance of a navy, seems obvious. Yet, as Hampden had previously held, he maintained again that this money would not have been under any sort of oversight by Parliament, even when it was in session—and it had not been for several years—plus the monies collected would basically constitute the King's own personal account. Hampden, Lord Saye and others additionally contended that there would in practice never be an end to the Ship Money tax; the King would always find a pretext for its imposition each and every year and could even increase revenues by raising the values on the taxed property.

Hampden, represented by Oliver St John, a cousin of Oliver Cromwell, was brought to trial on 6 November 1637, eventually losing in a judgment of seven to five. One of the five justices who found in his favor, fellow Buckinghamshire gentleman Sir George Croke, remarkably stated in his findings that as his guide in judging Hampden he relied solely on 'God's direction and my own conscience.' These were seen justifiably as ominous words considering the fact that the jurors were legally bound to decide the case according to the laws of the land, not according to their own personal biases or sense of personal direction from God. This abuse of the system made even Edward Hyde, then a member for Wootton Bassett, and later adviser to and mouthpiece of King Charles, extremely uneasy about the nature of the current government.[17]

Adair sums up the episode thus:

> (T)he nobility and gentry interpreted (Ship
> Money) as an attempt to overthrow the Constitu-
> tion of the Kingdom, and a threat to the concept
> of private property. Hampden lost the case and
> he duly paid the sum for which he had been
> assessed. But the King had won a Pyrrhic victory.

Adair adds an astute comment from Hyde that

> Hampden's carriage throughout that agitation
> was with that rare temper and modesty that
> they who watched him narrowly to find some
> advantage against his person, to make him less
> resolute in his cause, were compelled to give
> him a just testimony. And the judgement that
> was given against him infinitely more advanced
> him than the service for which it was given.[18]

Another event which would not soon be forgotten by
the Puritan faithful took place at about the time of
Hampden's 1637 trial. Barrister William Prynne, along
with minister Alexander Leighton and several other
men had been the force behind the printing of a tract
entitled *Sion's Plea against the Prelacy* which called for
the murder of all the bishops of the realm by the means
of spearing them 'under their fifth ribs'. (Piercing a
man's chest at the fifth rib, according to the Book of
Samuel in the Bible, is a way to cause certain, instanta-
neous death). Not surprisingly, Archbishop Laud made
an extreme example of these two men and their friends
by sending them to be judged in the Star Chamber and
sentencing them to be whipped, having their ears
cropped, their noses slit and their cheeks branded with
the mark 'SS'—denoting a 'Stirrer up of Sedition'.[19]

Despite the inflammatory and threatening language
in the pamphlet, the punishment was viewed as overly

harsh by many. Over time, the memory of the Prynne trial would combine unhappily with the memory of the Ship Money trial, and in the next Long Parliament, Charles would be made to regret this most recent use of judicial overkill.

Notes

1   http://www.thamehistory.net/placesGrammarschoolC17. htm.
2   *Parish Register of St Mary Magdalene, Great Hampden, Ed. By E.A. Ebblewhite* (Aylesbury: 1888), p. 10.
3   J. Adair, *A Life of John Hampden The Patriot 1594–1643* (London: MacDonald and Jane's, 1976), p. 141.
4   E. Hyde, Earl of Clarendon, *History of the Rebellion and Civil Wars in England, Ed. By W. D. Macray* (Oxford, 1888), p. 60.
5   A. Fraser, *Cromwell, The Lord Protector* (New York: Alfred A. Knopf, 1973), p. 213.
6   F. Hansford-Miller, *John Hampden — An Illustrated Life of John Hampden* (Aylesbury: Shire Publications, 1976), p. 26.
7   Adair, *A Life of John Hampden*, p. 53.
8   H. R. Williamson, *John Hampden, A Life* (London: Hodder & Stoughton, 1933), p. 105.
9   *Ibid.*, p. 195.
10 *Ibid.*, p. 130.
11 *Ibid.*, p. 115.
12 *Ibid.*, p. 115.
13 *Ibid.*, pp. 116, 117.
14 Fraser, *Cromwell*, p. 35.
15 Adair, *A Life of John Hampden*, p. 67.
16 F. Hansford-Miller, *John Hampden — An Illustrated Life of John Hampden*, p. 26.
17 P. Seaward, Preface to E. Hyde, Earl of Clarendon, *History of the Rebellion and Civil Wars in England, Ed. By W.D. Macray* (Oxford, 1888), p. ix.
18 Adair, *A Life of John Hampden*, p. 124.
19 *Ibid.*, p. 96.

10

PATRIAE PATER

HE INTERVENING YEARS between the last Parliament and the Short Parliament called on 15 April 1640 had seen yet another crisis, one which was building between Charles and the increasingly strict Calvinist churches in Scotland. The King was determined to force all Scots to adopt the English *Book of Common Prayer*, to kneel during worship, and join in general communion with the Church of England under the strict auspices of Archbishop Laud. The Scots, vehemently opposed to having any bishops whatsoever, believed this clearly violated their right to determine their form of worship and they made the radical move to totally abolish the episcopacy in 1639. In Churchill's words, the Scots now had 'a fanatical religious passion. The preachers, sword at side, carbine in hand, aided the drill sergeants with their exhortations.'[1] Tensions finally boiled over in May 1639, just after the dissolution when, impelled by Calvinist fervor, 25,000 Scottish troops crossed the Tweed into England.

The spectre of an English civil war haunted the mind of Sir Henry Slingsby, a Yorkshire gentleman living not far from the Scottish border, who wrote in his diary in 1639:

> These are strange, strange spectacles to see in this nation that have lived thus long peaceably, without noise of shot and drum and after we have stood neutrals and in peace when all the

world besides hath been in arms and wasted
with it, it is a thing I say most horrible that we
should engage ourself in a war with one
another, and with our own venom grow and
consume oneself.[2]

This first Scottish War was ended with the signing of
the Treaty of Berwick in 1639. Tensions remained
regarding all the previous unresolved issues; however,
historian Hugh Ross Williamson says of Hampden's
own conflicted views during the eleven years of
Charles' Personal Rule:

Hampden was too wise to mistake the bitterness
of his own heart for the temper of the country.
Eliot had died for an ideal—a course which many
might admire but few would emulate. Hampden
realized that, however certain he himself might
be of future strife, the men of England would
never be roused until the hardness of conditions
bred general discontent. Revolution, to be successful, depended on the existence of the many
coinciding with the effective leadership of the
few. It depended, moreover, on the existence of
a central rallying point which, until there was a
Parliament again, was lacking.[3]

Charles showed his clear inability to gauge the tem-
perature of the populace when he decided, after ten
years of Personal Rule, to call another sitting of Parliament. The elections which followed served only to
highlight the factionalism and general concern over
the abuse of royal power which had grown steadily
during all the years without the deliberative body.
Williamson described the dangerous progression of
the thought process of many Puritans during this time:

> Just as they had refused to imagine that they
> would be eternally damned for refusing to
> subscribe to the (Ship Money) loan, so now they
> doubted if incompetent government and illegal
> taxation were the authentic manifestations of
> the Divine Will.'[4]

It was immediately evident upon the first meeting of
the Short Parliament that all of the old issues remained
extant and would be revisited yet again. Unwilling to
live with the fact that, even if a new Ship Money
proposal passed, it was likely that members would
stipulate that none of the monies raised could be used
against Scotland, Charles decided to dissolve this sitting
of Parliament. On Wednesday 6 May 1640 Hampden,
Pym, the Earl of Warwick, Sir Walter Earle, Lord Saye
and Lord Brooke were arrested. A thorough search of
Hampden's person turned up no evidence of an alliance
with the Scots, however, and Hampden was released.

Due to the continuing unrest with the Scots, by
November Charles was forced to call another Parliament (in his words, 'to renew his acquaintance' with
the members!) even if the only outcome was to raise
funds for the military. In his speech in the House of
Lords, Charles assured Parliamentarians that he would
work with them on the many conflicts they had experienced in the past. The Commons then elected William
Lenthall as their Speaker, and the Puritan Parliamentarians lost no time in putting forth new legislation.

Believed to be the joint handiwork of Oliver
Cromwell, Arthur Heselrigge and Sir Henry Vane the
younger, the so-called 'Root and Branch' bill was
debated in the Spring of 1641. The bill aimed for no less
than the total abolition of the episcopacy although it also
included language abolishing Communion rails and

representations of the Virgin Mary in churches. The bill as a whole was abandoned but certain measures included in it did pass. Not easily dissuaded, Cromwell supported another bill calling for the abolition of Bishops in the House of Lords, which went down to defeat.[5]

By the time of this Long Parliament, John Pym and Hampden had together become popular leaders in the House of Commons. Pym, from Somerset, had been prominent in the 1628 charges laid against Roger Maynwaring and Charles Sibthorpe, two clergymen who had published sermons supporting the divine right of kings. Pym believed the publishing of the sermons was a sly attempt by Charles to encourage absolute monarchy, which would run counter to the English constitution.

Abhorred by the perceived treatment of Prynne and others over the course of many years, Pym was instrumental in the passing of the revolutionary Act of Habeas Corpus of 1641, in which the Star Chamber, the notorious tool of the Crown, was finally abolished. Originally meant to serve as a court for cases involving the titled or powerful who in the usual judicial system would realistically never be found guilty, the Chamber had evolved into a frightening instrument of the monarch in which the individual called before the justices could be found in contempt of court by simply refusing to answer a question. But even more disturbingly, individuals could be tried for 'crimes' which were not strictly crimes according to the law. In practice, anyone could be, and historically many had been, called before the court for acting contrary to the monarch's wishes. Undoubtedly the abolition of the Star Chamber was one of Pym's greatest achievements. Along with forcing the Crown to follow the letter of the law in charging people with crimes, the ending of the practice of forced self-incrimination served as a model for the Fifth Amendment of the American Constitution, both concepts being bulwarks of the American judicial system.

The Long Parliament wasted no time in attempting to further curb what they considered an out-of-touch and out-of-control monarchy. Lord Keeper Finch, the head justice who had been responsible for setting the seal of approval on the legality of the Ship Money tax, and who also had been bodily held down in his chair by Holles and Valentine in 1629, was finally impeached on 19 December 1640.

Next the Parliament under Pym passed the Triennial Act—which was paired with a subsidy bill so Charles had no option but to accept it—stating that only Parliament itself, not the Crown, had the right to dissolve a sitting of the body, a revolutionary concept for the time and one which must have greatly angered Charles, he who earlier had not seen fit to call a Parliament for almost eleven years.

Just days after the opening of the Long Parliament, another opportunity arose for Pym, Hampden and the rest of the Puritan contingent to further challenge the power of King Charles in the form of the Strafford affair. Thomas Wentworth, the Earl of Strafford, a member of Charles' Privy Council, had in his possession incriminating correspondence between Pym and the invading Scots which would be proof of a treasonable attempt to ally with the Presbyterians of Scotland against the English monarch.

Aware of this fact, Pym outmaneuvered Strafford by putting the Earl on trial first, using as evidence a purloined note ostensibly from a Privy Council discussion on the situation in Ireland. In language which would be justifiably shocking to most Englishmen, the note alluded to the idea that the King could use the Irish troops back in England to 'reduce' his own country and fight the Scottish forces. In the end, Parliament was successful in forcing Charles to sign Strafford's death warrant and having Strafford executed for treason, but a groundswell of conservative fellow-feeling for Charles gained much momentum as a result. Even some of the staunchest Puritans blanched at the utter humiliation of the King being forced to sign a death warrant for his closest friend.

In the ensuing years of this Parliament, Pym continued his mission to limit the power of the monarchy, well past the point where he began to alienate some in his Puritan fervor. In Adair's estimation, Pym was 'more a Leader of the House than a Prime Minister. The higher direction of affairs probably lay in Hampden's hands'. In contrast to Pym, Hyde wrote, 'Mr Hampden was a man of much greater cunning and it may be of the greatest address and insinuation to bring anything to pass which he desired of any man of that time, and who laid the design deepest.' In private conversations and meetings, he asserted, Pym was 'much governed' by Hampden ... thus Hampden may actually have been the true architect of the English Revolution.[6]

In contrast to his great friend Pym, Hampden won the hearts of the people by his easy manner and persuasive oratory. In the words of Edward Hyde,

> When this Parliament began, the eyes of all men were fixed on him as their *Patriae pater,* and the pilot that must steer their vessel through the tempests and rocks which threatened it. And I am persuaded his power and interest at that time was greater to do good or hurt than any

man's in the kingdom, or any man of his rank hath had in any time; for his reputation for honesty was universal, and his affections seemed so publicly guided that no corrupt or private ends could bias them. He was of that rare affability and temper in debate, and of that seeming humility and submission of judgment, as if he brought no opinions with him, but a desire of information and instruction; yet he had so subtle a way of interrogating, and under the notion of doubts insinuating his objections, that he left his opinions with those from whom he pretended to learn and receive them.[7]

In the end, Churchill writes,

The excesses and fanaticism of the Puritan party, their war upon the Church, their confederacy with the Scottish invaders, roused antagonisms ... from which the Crown might by patience and wisdom emerge ... henceforward the quarrel was no longer between the King and the People but between the two main themes and moods of conservatism vs. radicalism which continue down to the present day.[8]

In Williamson's view, the stalemate ground on through this last difficult prewar year while

(N)either side wished to be the first to appeal directly to arms. Charles hoped by foreign aid to intimidate the country, and by arresting and executing their leaders to break the Commons. The Commons struggled to protect themselves by gaining the right to arm the people of England if necessity arose. Thus began the maneuvrings for position, during which both King and Commons remained as far as they could within the letter of irrelevant and outworn laws.[9]

Notes

[1]   W. L. Churchill, *The History of the English-Speaking Peoples, Arranged for One Volume by Henry Steele Commager* (New York: Dodd, Mead & Co., 1956), p. 176.

[2]   A. Fraser, *Cromwell, The Lord Protector* (New York: Alfred A. Knopf, 1973), p. 58.

[3]   H. R. Williamson, *John Hampden, A Life* (London: Hodder & Stoughton, 1939), p. 167.

[4]   J. Adair, *A Life of John Hampden The Patriot 1594–1643* (London: MacDonald and Jane's. 1976), p. 140.

[5]   Fraser, *Cromwell*, p. 70.

[6]   Williamson, *John Hampden*, p. 116.

[7]   E. Hyde, Earl of Clarendon, *History of the Rebellion and Civil Wars in England, Ed. By W. D. Macray* (Oxford: 1888), p. 172.

[8]   Churchill, *The History of the English-Speaking Peoples*, p. 180.

[9]   Williamson, *John Hampden*, p. 279.

11

'I HAVE NOT EYES TO SEE'

N THE AUTUMN of 1641 Parliament, fed up with new rumors that the King was secretly arranging with Holland and Denmark for war materiel in case hostilities broke out, drew up what became known as 'The Grand Remonstrance'. In this statement the Commons charged the monarch with attempting to 'subvert the fundamental laws and principles of government upon which the religion and justice of the kingdom was established.'[1]

Together with a list of grievances against the Crown that dated back to 1632 with Sir John Eliot's death in the Tower, the members presented a contrasting list of accomplishments of the present Parliament, such as the victory against Ship Money and against the arbitrary power of the Crown to tax subjects. The Remonstrance also included a future plan for the King to reform the entire Church of England bishopric, removing all temporal power from bishops and stripping certain ceremonies from Church practice.

In *The History of the English-Speaking Peoples* Winston Churchill relates a scene which took place in 1641 in the House of Commons when John Pym, representing Somerset, presented the bill. In a conversation between Oliver Cromwell, John Hampden's first cousin, and Lucius Cary, Viscount Falkland, Cromwell is quoted as saying as they left the House 'If the Remonstrance had been rejected I would have sold all that I had (the) next morning, and never had seen England any more; and I know there are many honest men of the same resolution.' In his version of this event, Hyde bemoans the outcome, adding 'So near was the poor kingdom at that time to its deliverance!'[2] Churchill observed,

> He, and Pym also, looked across the ocean to new lands where the cause for which they were prepared to die, or kill, could breathe, albeit in a wilderness. Their sentiments awoke echoes in America that were not to be stilled until more than a century later, and after much bloodshed.[3]

The Remonstrance had passed in the small hours of the morning, and Hampden then suggested that the bill be printed—and therefore available to the populace to read—an action which may have created an insurrection all on its own. Members who had voted against the bill were aghast at the idea, and swords were drawn and at the ready. Hampden himself gave a brief speech which not only cooled down the hot tempers of those who believed they had the backing of the majority to fight the printing of the Remonstrance, but did much to add to his growing reputation for statesmanship.

In his turn, Charles made a perfunctory promise to call a synod of the Church of England, but no further developments came from the Remonstrance. However, he was just biding his time, for by 3 January 1642, the King finally charged Lord Mandeville, Pym, Hampden, Denzil Holles, Sir Arthur Heselrigge and William Strode with high treason on the basis of

> Casting aspersions on the King and his government, encouraging the Scots to invade England, raising tumults to coerce Parliament, levying war against the King, and trying to subvert the

fundamental laws of and government of the Kingdom.[4]

In what must be seen in any light as a very under-handed move, Charles suddenly removed the guard which was responsible for protecting the Houses of Parliament[5] and on 4 January the King, to the general amazement of the crowds lining the streets, began a procession from Whitehall toward Westminster accompanied by approximately 500 armed Cavalier bodyguards. He was on a mission to seize the five men, sent with more than a blessing by his Queen, Henrietta, who it is said admonished him before he left the palace: 'Pull the rogues out by the ears.'[6] Fortunately Pym had received advance word from the Countess of Carlisle, a lady-in-waiting to the Queen,[7] and he and the other four members were able to make their escape to the City by boat at Parliament stairs.

Thirty minutes later the King stood silhouetted at the door of St Stephen's Chapel. He did not go so far as to allow his armed retainers to enter, but he strode in brazenly, bowing to the members as they in turn bowed to him, and he walked all the way to the Speaker's chair. It undoubtedly must have been an astonishing experience as the members watched the English monarch approach the Speaker of the House of Commons and to hear him announce

> Mr Speaker, I must for a time make bold with your chair ... Gentlemen, I am sorry to have this occasion to come unto you. Yesterday, I sent a sergeant at arms to demand some who, by my order, were accused of high treason. Instead of obedience I received a message. I must here declare to you, that though no king that ever was in England could be more careful of your

> privileges than I shall be, yet in cases of treason
> no person has privilege … I must have these
> men wheresoever I can find them.[8]

Lenthall stepped down from the Speaker's seat, turned toward Charles and knelt, hat doffed and head bowed, before the King who had appropriated his chair. Charles then asked if Lenthall would point out the five members charged with treason. To his everlasting credit, and belying his later spineless vacillation as Speaker, Lenthall calmly replied to the King,

> Sire, I have not eyes to see nor lips to speak in
> this place except as the members of this House
> direct me, whose servant I am here, and humbly
> beg Your Majesty's pardon, that I cannot give
> any other answer than this to what Your
> Majesty is pleased to demand of me.[9]

Men throughout the history of England had been thrown in the Tower, never to be seen again, for much less of an affront to a king. 'No matter,' Charles nonchalantly replied, 'I have eyes well enough of my own' and he proceeded to glare at each of the members, attempting to recognize the five men from amongst the assembly. After the passage of several minutes Charles stated, 'I perceive my birds have flown.'

Then after a moment he added,

> I do expect that you shall send them unto me
> as soon as they return hither. If not, I will seek
> them myself, for their treason is foul. I assure
> you, on the word of a King, I never did intend
> any force, but shall proceed against them in a
> legal and fair way, for I never meant any other.[10]

He then walked back through the now-standing members, many of whom were shouting 'Privilege! Privilege!'

at him as he passed, in outrage that a sovereign could dare violate the sanctity of the House of Commons.[11]

'Speaker Lenthall asserting the privilege of the Commons against Charles I when the attempt was made to seize the Five Members' by Charles West Cope.
Palace of Westminster Collection

Such consternation and shock ensued in both Houses after this episode that Robert Devereux, the Earl of Essex, immediately proposed that the House of Lords work as intermediaries between the King and the accused members. Unfortunately nothing came of the idea.[12]

Historian David Hume related sadly that the King had retreated to Hampton Court 'overwhelmed with grief, shame and remorse for the fatal measures into which he had been hurried … his own precipitancy and indiscretion must bear the blame of whatever disasters should henceforth befall him.'[13]

Yet strictly speaking, legally the King was justified in his actions. As set forth by Hume, there was no actual law, only custom, which forbade a monarch from entering the Commons when there is a question of a member committing 'treason, felony or breach of peace; nor has either house, during former ages, ever pretended, in any of those cases, to interpose in behalf of its members.'[14] In light of this unavoidable reality, we must view the actions and exclamations of outrage of those in Commons that day as a result of the long-simmering anger encouraged, many times justifiably, by Parliament and the Puritan party against the King—or his much-maligned 'advisers', who usually took the brunt of the criticism instead of the actual institution of the monarchy or the person of the King. Clearer heads did not prevail that day inside the House, nor outside of it, as one of the assembled crowd through which Charles walked shouted audibly to him, 'To your tents, O Israel!' in a clear incitement to the people to rebel against their King just as the ancient Israelites had done against their leader Rehoboam.

For several days the Commons met in different locations around the City, including the Grocers' Hall, guarded by the Parliamentarian trained-bands which had sprung up about London. It wasn't until Tuesday 11 January that the members felt safe enough to return to Westminster, when Hampden and the other four members came out of their hiding place on Coleman Street and were rowed back the way they had come a week earlier, passing by many gaily-decorated gun boats that were lining the Thames in a show of support for the Parliamentary cause.[15]

This tempestuous episode proved once for all to a populace that was all too eager to assume the worst that the King was not to be trusted to respect their rights. Charles, hounded out of the capital, never set foot as a free man in London after that day. Several days later a petition signed and delivered by Hampden's Buckinghamshire constituents was received by the King at Hampton Court. Charles had to look upon the sight of six thousand men, each with a copy of the Remonstrance stuck in his hatband, as they read their petition. The document stated that they were there in support of 'John Hampden, knight of our shire, in whose loyalty we, his countrymen and neighbors, have ever had good cause to confide; of late we, to our no less amazement than grief, find him accused of treason.' Charles wisely realized whether or not he had been in the right when he entered the chamber, there was little to gain by further inflaming the Commons, and he agreed to lay aside all charges for the present.[16]

In the January elections for London, the pendulum of power swung toward Parliament, as the city now vowed allegiance to Parliament and Pym.[17] The entire kingdom began quickly to devolve into armed camps, with Parliament and its trained-bands newly pronouncing loyalty to the Army, attempting to gain control of it and its supplies; and Charles meanwhile maneuvering with foreign powers to shore up his Cavaliers' strength if and when hostilities broke out.

In Hume's view,

> (T)he fears and jealousies which operated on the people, and pushed them so furiously to arms were undoubtedly not of a civil, but of a religious nature. The distempered imaginations of men were agitated with a continual dread of Popery, with a horror against prelacy, with an antipathy to ceremonies and the liturgy, and with a violent affection for whatever was most

opposite to these objects of aversion. The fanatical spirit, let loose, confounded all regard to ease, safety, interest; and dissolved every moral and civil obligation.[18]

Notes

1 J. Adair, *A Life of John Hampden The Patriot 1594–1643* (London: MacDonald and Jane's, 1976), p. 159.
2 E. Hyde, Earl of Clarendon, *History of the Rebellion and Civil Wars in England, Ed. By W.D. Macray* (Oxford, 1888), p. 95.
3 W. L Churchill, *The History of the English-Speaking Peoples, Arranged for One Volume by Henry Steele Commager* (New York: Dodd, Mead & Co., 1956), p. 182.
4 Adair, *A Life of John Hampden,* p. 164.
5 H. R. Williamson, *John Hampden, A Life* (London: Hodder & Stoughton, 1933), p. 280.
6 *Ibid.,* p. 283.
7 D. Hume, *History of England,* (New York: Harper and Brothers, 1868) vol v, p. 207.
8 *Ibid.,* p. 207.
9 *Ibid,* p. 207.
10 Williamson, *John Hampden,* pp. 285, 286.
11 Adair, *A Life of John Hampden,* p. 165.
12 Hyde, *History of the Rebellion,* p. 117.
13 Hume, *History of England,* p. 210.
14 *Ibid.,* p. 210.
15 F. Hansford-Miller, *John Hampden — An Illustrated Life of John Hampden* (Aylesbury: Shire Publications, 1976), pp. 34–35.
16 *Ibid.,* p. 36.
17 V. Pearl, *London and the Outbreak of Puritan Revolution, City Government and National Politics 1625–1643* (Oxford University Press, 1961), p. 3.
18 Hume, *History of England,* p. 220.

12

No Way Back

OR THE NEXT several months, well into the Spring of 1642, Parliament and the Crown continually disputed the issues that were rendering the Kingdom asunder. No compromises were reached on any of the main points of contention. By the first of June Parliament presented a list of nineteen 'Propositions to the King' which amounted to a boldfaced demand that Charles relinquish complete control over both state and church affairs, an act which—similar to the earlier Strafford affair—struck such a tone of brazen impunity that it inadvertently strengthened Royalist sentiments.

In general, the 'Old England' of the nobility was in Charles' camp although many nobles did sympathize with Pym and the Puritans. The tradesmen and merchants, some of whose apprentices wore the bowl-shaped haircut that gave them the name Roundheads, supported Parliament in the main. Geographically the kingdom was split into a north and west that generally were Royalist while counties closest to London favored Parliament.

Still, the Puritans' main aim was truly not to destroy the monarchy as such, but rather, in true Puritan form, to 'rescue' or separate Charles from his 'evil counsellors', which no doubt included any and all Catholic and Church of England connections he had, including Archbishop Laud.[1] For his part, according to Churchill, 'Charles vowed himself to live as a constitutional monarch, adhering to the laws of the realm.' And perhaps most disturbing of all was that this was a series of conflicts which pitted brother against brother in a land in which families already were deeply divided along religious lines in many cases. Churchill notes,

> Behind all class and political issues the religious quarrel was the driving power. In Cromwell's words, 'Religion was not the thing at first contested for, but God brought it to that issue at last … it proved that which was most dear to us.'[2]

Hampden was instrumental in passing the Militia Ordinance in the spring of 1642 which called for each county to organize men for defence. For his part, Hampden together with Arthur Goodwin headed up the 'Greencoats' of Buckinghamshire (the 20th) while Denzil Holles had the 'Redcoats' of London (the 13th), Lord Saye was the head of the 'Bluecoats' of Oxfordshire (the 9th) and Lord Brooke headed the 'Purplecoats' (the 6th) from Warwickshire. Hampden took as the motto for his own regiment '*Vestigia nulla retrorsum*' ('No way back'); in tribute to its native son, the county of Buckinghamshire later adopted this phrase as its motto.[3]

A friend and neighbor of Hampden's, Sir Edmund Verney, was chosen to be the keeper of the Royal Standard. For Verney, the way forward was not tortuous but perfectly clear. Nothing came before his loyalty to Charles. In speaking to Hyde, Verney stated, 'I do not like the quarrel and do heartily wish that the King would yield and consent to what they desire. My conscience only is concerned in honor and in gratitude to follow my master. I have eaten his bread and served him nearly thirty years, and will not do so base a thing as forsake him; and choose rather to lose my life—

which I am sure to do—to preserve and defend those things that are against my conscience to preserve and defend.'[4]

Hampden still undoubtedly was able psychologically to sever the person of Charles from the office of King of England, as we have proof from the engraved saying on the silver pendant he was to wear around his neck in battle:

> Against my King I do not fight
> But for my King and Kingdom's right.

As Williamson states,

> (I)f, in his mind, he still distinguished the man Charles Stuart from the King of England, the person from the office—as the Parliamentary declaration had done—the distinction was subtle enough to invite the charge of casuistry. Yet ... treason was a sin; to Verney, the greatest; to Hampden, only less than treachery to conscience.[5]

In a similar, tragic vein, in a June 1643 letter to his old friend Ralph Hopton, Colonel Sir William Waller, leader of four regiments of horse and two of dragoons, eloquently expressed the exquisite moral dilemma in which the sons of England found themselves during the terrible years of strife:

> That great God which is the searcher of my heart, knows with what a sad sense I go upon this service, and with what a perfect hatred I detest this war without an enemy, but I look upon it as '*opus domini*', which is enough to silence all passion in me. The God of peace in his good time will send us peace, and in the mean time fit us to receive it. We are both upon the stage and must act these parts that are assigned to us in

> this tragedy. Let us do it in a way of honour, and
> without personal animosities.[6]

Upon the inexorable complete breakdown of his relationship with Parliament, Charles raised the royal
standard at Nottingham and called his loyal subjects to
him in August 1642, making his nephew Prince Rupert
Commander General of Horse; the Earl of Lindsey
General; and Sir Jacob Astley Major-General of Foot.
Robert Devereux, the Earl of Essex, was named Lord
General of the Parliamentarian armies. The two armies
were unequal in every way, but the Roundheads made
up for their lack of training with their fighting spirit.

Lansdowne proved a victory for Charles, as was
Bristol, then the second-largest English city, where
warships in the port declared their loyalty to the
Crown. Edgehill, in October, marked the first major
battle for Captain Oliver Cromwell under the partial
leadership of his cousin, the new Colonel John Hampden. Hampden came late to the battle, having led a
train of artillery to the site and arriving with a brigade
of his own Greencoats added to Colonel Thomas
Grantham's and Lord Willoughby's regiments. The
Parliamentarian forces combined with Cromwell's
men and met Prince Rupert's troops at the town of
Kineton, which was in danger of being looted by the
Royalists already in residence there.[7] The Edgehill
contest ended in a draw overall, but before long
Charles was marching into Oxford in triumph, with
the Parliamentarian army marching southeast toward
London, harried all the while by the King's cavalry.

At Brentford, just west of the capital, the forces
clashed again on 12 November, joined by Colonel
Hampden's Greencoats and the remains of Lord
Brooke's regiment, but the Royalists held the town and

continued to march eastward. One mile further on they met the full force of the Parliamentarian and City of London massed troops, comprising a force of 24,000 mixed apprentices and army regimental soldiers. Perhaps due to strategic or tactical errors on the part of Essex, no further advances were made against the King's arrayed forces. The next day Charles decided to pull back, basing the men for the most part in Oxford and Reading.

It wasn't until the beginning of the next year, on 19 January, when the armies saw significant action again, as local Parliamentarian forces at Braddock Downs, Devon, were bested by the volunteer Royal regiments led by the Marquess of Hertford.[8] By April, Reading had become the focus of the two armies after Oxford remained in Royalist possession. The Parliamentarians took Caversham Hill outside Reading and were successful in bombarding and toppling the tower of Caversham Church, where the Royalists had 'mounted two light guns' according to Adair.[9] The next day Lord Grey of Wark, together with troops and materiel from the new Eastern Association, joined in the siege of the city.

Two Cavalier regiments, the Green and the Red, attacked and fought seemingly to a draw, yet the governor of Reading sued the Royalist forces for surrender. Lord General Essex in the end gave up much of the materiel he had just received from the Eastern Association, which caused morale to sink in the Parliamentarian ranks. Even Hampden's Green-coat Regiment (most of whom were Bucks men and his constituents) refused to march out of Reading without their back pay, and did not move until they were spoken to by Hampden himself.

Essex, under pressure from Parliamentarians in London to effect some sort of meaningful action, decided to move against the Cavaliers in Oxfordshire. In addition to routing out the Royalist cavalry that was ensconced throughout neighboring Buckinghamshire, Essex meant to intercept a shipment of war materiel sent by Queen Henrietta which he had learned was on its way south toward Oxford. He amassed his own three thousand pikemen and musketeers outside Wallingford in early June, and together with Colonel Morley's regiment of horse and companies of dragoons, the total Parliamentary force most likely amounted to 15,000 men.[10]

In another reminder of how closely interwoven were the lives of these men during the Wars, Essex had his headquarters in Thame, Oxfordshire, the very town where Hampden and William Lenthall, and possibly the Reverend Robert Lenthall as well, had attended grammar school together as boys. In all likelihood, his forces would have gone past or through Great Haseley, Little Haseley and Latchford, the home of the Lenthalls, on their way to the battle of Chalgrove in June, as those villages would have been the closest places in which to find forage and provisions for the armies. Significant sustenance had already undoubtedly been given to the Royalist cause in March 1643 when Prince Rupert's troops marched through the Haseleys on their way to Henley.[11] Additionally, in 1644, months after the Royalist victory at Chalgrove, yet more aid was given to the Cavaliers when grain from the parish was given to the Royalist garrison at Oxford.[12]

Perhaps the furnishing of the Parliamentary army's requirements in June 1643, as the Roundhead troops headed toward Chalgrove, was the reason behind the leniency with which the villages were treated after the Restoration. The Wray family, of Rycote, near Latchford, which had even been fined during the Interregnum for assisting the Royals, were allowed to keep their lands, as were all other landowners of the parish.[13] But perhaps some dealing was done behind the scenes, as Speaker Lenthall may well have used what influence he had garnered to beg for mercy for his relatives and fellow landowners of the area.

Notes

[1]   W. L. Churchill, *The History of the English-Speaking Peoples, Arranged for One Volume by Henry Steele Commager* (New York: Dodd, Mead & Co., 1956), p. 183.

[2]   *Ibid.,* p. 183.

[3]   H. R. Williamson, *John Hampden, A Life* (London: Hodder & Stoughton, 1933, pp. 299, 301.

[4]   *Ibid.,* pp. 302, 303.

[5]   *Ibid.,* p. 303.

[6]   J. Adair, *A Life of John Hampden, the Patriot 1594–1643* (London: MacDonald and Jane's, 1976), p. 225.

[7]   *Ibid.,* p. 192.

[8]   *Ibid.,* p. 208.

[9]   *Ibid.,* p. 217.

[10] *Ibid.,* p. 226.

[11] I. G. Philip (ed.), *Journal of Sir Samuel Luke,* I (ORS 29, 1950), p. 25; II (ORS 31,1951), pp. 96, 98.

[12] M. Toynbee (ed.), *Papers of Captain Henry Stevens* (ORS 42, 1962), 33; *Cal. Committee for Advance of Money,* I, p. 237.

[13] *HMC Ormonde MSS VII,* pp. 163–4; *Wood's Life,* III, pp. 54, 135, 152; *VCH Oxon.* IV, p. 123.

13

'A QUIET CONSCIENCE AND A NATION'S LOVE'

O N SUNDAY MORNING 18 June Colonel Hampden arranged his troops, together with those of Major John Gunter and Captain James Sheffield, and swung toward the southwest, harrying Prince Rupert's Life-guards and Regiment of Horse as they all drove toward Chalgrove. Although with only a quarter of the soldiers the Royalists had at their command, once he reached Chalgrove Field Hampden moved westward, following Prince Rupert, as the Prince possibly made a tactical retreat to entice Hampden into a skirmish. Hampden for his part may have been trying to engage Rupert's men until the rest of Essex's forces appeared. Regardless of the intent, at one point shots were fired near a hedgerow where dragoons were lined up. The Prince wheeled his horse about and charged through the hedgerow, and the Battle of Chalgrove Field began.

Rupert led his Life-guards in an attack on the left wing of the Parliamentarians while General Percy and Major Daniel added the strength of their troops against Hampden. It was not long until, according to Adair, Hampden suffered his mortal wound when a Cavalier 'had ridden up and shot him from behind with a double-loaded carbine or pistol.'[1] Meanwhile, the Royalists broke through what was left of the Parliamentarian ranks and made the most of their huge advantage in numbers, driving the smaller force, now minus the thirty Parliamentarian troops killed that day at Chalgrove, over Golder Hill in complete retreat.

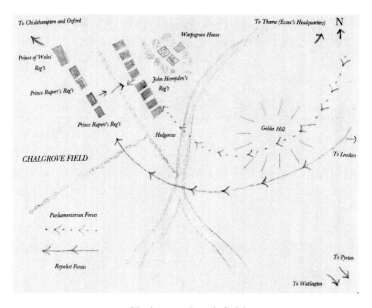

Chalgrove Battlefield

Bleeding profusely, even through his coat, Hampden was seen leaving the field, propping himself up by leaning on his horse's neck, and reportedly riding in the direction of Pyrton Manor, where his first, beloved wife Elizabeth had lived as a girl. He was forced to turn back, however, when he saw the area was thick with Royalist troops. In a sad refutation of the meaning of Hampden's regimental motto *Vestigia nulla retrorsum*, Hampden found himself indeed tragically finding his way back, but instead of retracing the steps he had ridden on his way to woo Elizabeth many years prior, he found his way back to his old school town of Thame. In Williamson's words,

> Twenty-four years ago, on just such a day,
> though with the cornfields untrammeled by war
> and the meadows at peace under the heat-haze,
> he had ridden lightheartedly to Elizabeth at
> Pyrton to make the final plans for their wedding.
> It wanted but six days to the anniversary of it.[2]

He rode a full five miles back to Thame, where he finally found respite and care for his wound at the home of a man named Ezekiel Browne.

He lay gravely wounded for several days at the Browne home (which later became the Greyhound Inn). Although the bullet was recovered immediately from his shoulder, as the week progressed Hampden began to suffer from a fever, or possibly gangrene. Hampden, *Patriae pater* and warrior without an enemy, died on Saturday, 24 June, at 48 years of age.

His friend Arthur Goodwin had been at Hampden's bedside at the Greyhound Inn, and after his death wrote the following in a letter to his daughter, Lady Wharton:

> I am here at Hampden in doing the last duty for
> the deceased owner of it, of whom every honest
> man hath a share in the loss, and will likewise
> in the sorrow. Truly Jenny … he was a gallant
> man, an honest man, an able man, and take all,
> I know not to any man living second … I would
> we all lay it to heart, that God takes away the
> best amongst us.[3]

An anonymous broadsheet published just after Hampden's death contains the following poem:

> But—noble soul—his purer thoughts were free
> From all corruption; he not valued friends
> A fair estate nor self-propounded ends
> Any preferment, nor aught else above
> A quiet conscience and his nation's love.[4]

Edward Hyde had keenly observed Hampden as he had made the transition from statesman to warrior; in his *History of the Rebellion*, he wrote:

> After he was amongst those members accused by the King of high treason, he was much altered, his nature and carriage seeming much fiercer than it did before. And without question, when he first drew the sword he threw away the scabbard for he passionately opposed the overture made by the King for a treaty from Nottingham, and, as eminently, any expedients that might have produced an accommodation in this ...[5]

But in summing up his character after his death, Hyde, though now a Royalist to the marrow, wrote generously of Hampden's loss:

> Never was there such consternation and sorrow over one man's death, as when tidings thereof did reach London, in the Parliament and the people throughout the land; as if their whole army had been defeated: his private loss is unspeakable.[6]

Hampden's body was borne back to Hampden House and his second wife Letitia and his surviving children Richard, William, Anne, Ruth and Mary. His first wife Elizabeth had died, most likely in childbirth, in 1634. His eldest son died at the beginning of the war and his eldest daughter succumbed at about the same time, in childbirth. The Reverend Robert Lenthall, newly returned from the American colonies and serving the family as the rector of St Mary Magdalene at Great Hampden, was there as well.

The 1647 book *A Worthy Discourse* written by the chaplain to Hampden's regiment relates the moving scene of Hampden's return:

> The body was received at the church by Master Robert Lenthall, minister of the parish of Great Hampden, and followed by no small company of soldiers, country folk and gentry; the pall being borne of six; viz Colonel Arthur Goodwin, Mr Richard Greenville (Sheriff of the county), Mr Tyrrell, Mr West, and Dr Giles (minister of Chinnor) and myself William Spurstow: the last named (Dr Giles) having been with the deceased Colonel at Thame in Oxfordshire during the days in which he languished of his hurt received in the fight near Chalgrove and at his death.[7]

Knowing full well that Hampden's remains could be desecrated by Royalist forces if he was buried in the chancel next to his late wife, I believe Robert buried Hampden himself, either outside in a nearby field, or perhaps immured elsewhere in St Mary Magdalene church, effectively hiding his friend's body forever. The parish register of the church shows Hampden as buried at the church, and the handwriting in the register is identical to other entries from 1643, although due to the turbulent events of that year, Lenthall was not officially installed as rector until 30 November of 1643.

As the editor of the St Mary Magdalene Parish Register stated,

> Much controversy has taken place respecting this entry, and at times its authenticity has been doubted. Although it must be admitted that the line (regarding Hampden's burial) has the appearance of an interpolation, it will be seen, on careful examination, that the handwriting is identical with the other burials of 1643. Robert Lenthall was formally inducted on the 30th November, and has recorded this fact prior to the

record of the Patriot's and other burials which took place earlier in the year. As I have stated … this Rector had no doubt officiated on these occasions, though, owing to the troublous times, he had not entered the fact until later in the year.[8]

Alongside the list of parish rectors in the register are anonymous notes written over the years which refer to Robert and his burial of Hampden:

Robert Lenthall (a supposed Relation of ye Speaker's) was inducted 30 Nov 1643 though, it is evident, from the entries on page 77, that he had been in charge of the parish for some months previous, and he officiated at the burial of the Patriot on the 25th of June, 1643.[9]

In 1828, George Grenville, Lord Nugent, as part of the research for his work *Some Memorials of John Hampden, His Party and his Times*, took it upon himself to exhume bodies from coffins buried inside St Mary Magdalene. Nugent primarily was interested in proving his theory that Hampden was killed by a pistol that had misfired and exploded in his hand, not, as had been rumored, a shot to the back of the shoulder by the Cavalier soldier. Lord Nugent, after examining several coffins and sets of remains, found that it was most likely not even the actual body of John Hampden buried near the memorial plaque for his first wife Elizabeth, but was most likely his father William. Much contradictory information has been bruited about regarding the exhumation, from the physical appearance and condition of the bodies in the coffins to whether or not the shoulder and wrist joints of one of them were actually broken (as would be expected with Hampden's wounds). The precise location of John Hampden's body has not been found to this day.[10]

In short, the Reverend Lenthall may have been the only person to ever know exactly where Hampden was buried, and Lenthall's secret went to the grave with him. Perhaps as a partial gesture of thanks owed Hampden for all that the great man had done for Lenthall in welcoming him back to Buckinghamshire and giving him the living of the family church, the rector took it upon himself to hide the body so extraordinarily well that it would never be found.

And just as Lenthall had feared, at the time of the Restoration in 1660, the new Parliament ordered the exhumation and hanging of the bodies of Oliver Cromwell, John Bradshaw and Henry Ireton as punishment and a warning for all regicides, and the heads of the three men were displayed on a spike above Westminster Hall. (Bradshaw had presided over the trial of Charles I and Ireton was Cromwell's son-in-law and had been a general in the Irish campaign). It was only after the passage of another seventeen years that Cromwell's skull fell down from its perch, having been swept off by a gale.

A total of twenty Parliamentarians who had died over the years of the Commonwealth, and who had been in some cases buried with great pomp in Westminster Abbey, had their corpses dug up and buried in a common pit near St Margaret's Church near the Abbey. However, the toll of those actually executed by the Crown was less than twelve, a number which had been with good reason feared to be much higher. The political climate at the time called for such extreme and public punishments, and Charles showed wisdom in acceding to the public's wishes while at the same time sparing the lives of many others who had rebelled. It is difficult for the modern reader not to feel pity for this monarch who was heard to say, at the end of the state-imposed executions, 'I am weary of hanging.'[11]

After giving his life at age forty-nine for his country and for the cause he believed in, at least John Hampden and his family were spared this desecration by his old friend and Puritan brother in spirit.

Aerial Photo of Great Hampden, showing Hampden House and St Mary Magdalene. Courtesy of the John Hampden Society

Notes

1   J. Adair, *A Life of John Hampden*, The *Patriot 1594–1643* (London: MacDonald and Jane's, 1976), p. 236.
2   H. R. Williamson, *John Hampden, A Life* (London: Hodder & Stoughton, 1933), p. 328.
3   Adair, *A Life of John Hampden*, p. 243.
4   F. Hansford-Miller, *John Hampden—An Illustrated Life of John Hampden* (Aylesbury: Shire Publications, 1976), p. 44.

5   E. Hyde, Earl of Clarendon, *The History of the Rebellion and Civil Wars in England, Ed. By W. D. Macray,* (Oxford: 1888), p. 173.

6   Adair, *A Life of John Hampden,* p. 245.

7   W. Spurstowe, Tract Entitled *True and Faithful Relation of a Worthy Discourse Between Colonel John Hampden and Colonel Oliver Cromwell, 1647* (London: Forgotten Books, 2013 from 1847 Reprint. Reprinted from The Patriot #60 Aylesbury: The John Hampden Society, 2013).

8   *Parish Register of St Mary Magdalene , Great Hampden, Ed. By E. A. Ebblewhite* (Aylesbury: 1888) p. 10.

9   *Ibid.,* Index Notes.

10 D. Lester and G. Blackshaw, *The Controversy of John Hampden's Death* (Oxfordshire: Chalgrove Battle Group, 2000), p. 33.

11 W. L. Churchill, *The History of the English-Speaking Peoples, Arranged for One Volume by Henry Steele Commager* (New York, Dodd, Mead & Co., 1956), p. 207.

14

THE UNIMAGINABLE

OR THE NEXT four years Robert Lenthall continued as rector, settling in after his years of
turmoil in New England and the loss of his
old friend, and enjoying the quiet living of Great
Hampden with Susanna and the two youngest children. By 1647 their only son Adrian was twenty years
of age; his younger sister Sarah was fourteen, and a
young cousin, John Pickering, had joined the family
while the two eldest children continued living with
their aunt and uncle in Connecticut.

During the summer of 1647 there had been an outbreak of the bubonic plague in England, not as widespread as some previous incidences, but rather localized
in certain areas. Sarah Lenthall had been staying with a
friend in London and planned to visit her family for only
one day, then return to the city again. In the margins of
the Great Hampden parish register, located now at the
county records office in Aylesbury, there is a note,
written by an unknown churchman years after the fact,
which apparently was meant to convey the horror the
church official had felt when he himself had read the
records from 1647. The note draws the reader's attention
to 'ye dreadfull & uncommon Fate of his (Robert's)
whole family in ye year, ye Register & in his own
handwriting'. Indeed Robert himself had inscribed the
following harrowing paragraphs in entries during
August and September of that year:

My daughter Sarah Lenthall was buried ye eleventh day of August ... she came from London to Wycombe and on the Saturday only, to see us and so to return tomorrow in the afternoon to Wycombe again, but then fell sick and on the Wednesday morning following being the 11th of August; an hour before sunrise died of sickness and so in the evening we buried her in the mead called the kitchen-mead by the hedge side as you go down into it on your left hand ... she was aged 14 years, eleven months and seventeen days—had she (lived) to Bartholomew's Day she had been full 15 years of age.

Susanna Lenthall my wife dep'ted this life Thursday evening about eight o'clock the 26th of August, she died of the sickness comfortably and in peace and was buried the 27th day by her daughter Sarah.

Adria(n) Lenthall my son a hopeful young man and near one and twenty years of age dep'ted this life of ye sickness, Thursday morning, a little before daybreak and was buried at the head of his sister's grave same day, being the 2nd of September.

My cousin John Pickering a lad about 13 years of age, dying of the sickness, was buried the 25th of September, 1647.

Robert Lenthall, Rector[1]

This unspeakable loss, added to the constant turmoil and confrontation of Robert's colonial years, could have driven a less faithful man to absolute despair. The unimaginable heartbreak of having to bury one's family, one member at a time, would have been almost unendurable for most men who did not believe in a heaven in which they would all be united together again. Lenthall did have his two eldest girls (Marianne was approximately eleven years of age and Ann nine) in Connecticut for solace, and doubtless he thanked God that they remained free of this scourge, though they certainly faced many other dangers and trials in the North American colonies of the 1640s.

Somehow Robert was able to return to the ministry although he made a change of scene, moving to Barnes in what was then Surrey, to the parish of St Mary's in 1649. He married for a second time to Cicely Gey, at High Wycombe, Buckinghamshire. She unfortunately also passed away soon afterward, and Robert buried her on 15 July 1650.[2] They had no children together.

Though he had no children left to survive him in England, Robert left living reminders of his life in 1652 when he planted three ash trees and four elms in St Mary's churchyard. He recorded the planting of the seven trees solemnly in the parish register; such a formal act might lead one to think perhaps each tree was planted to signify each of the five family members he had lost in England, plus two to represent his two daughters in Connecticut whom he would never see again. Whatever their significance, all the trees enjoyed remarkably long lives, being depicted several times throughout the years in sketches of the church; two trees survived into the 1900s and one of them lived until 1977.[3]

He continued to serve as rector at Barnes, and he even remarried for a third time, to a Margaret Barmston, and they remained together until Robert's death in September of 1658. There were no children from that marriage either, and his will, which has become fairly well-known in New England for some of its language addressed to his daughters, deals primarily with Margaret:

And my bodie I leave to my wife and children to see privately without any ringing or trouble of company interred in the churchyard of the parish church of Barnes.

Then, referring to books and other belongings,

my wife to have the first choice and then Marrian the second and Nan the third praying that this divident of my goods or whatsoever unbequeathed and to be divided betwixt them in money or goods may be done without Jar-ringe mumurynge discontent or unthankfulness on either part. And withall charging my two daughters to go content with that they have and not to give their mother anie inst cause of complaint against them, but to be respective to her and rather to receive wrong with patience than in any thinge to doe her the least injury or suffering to be done to her ... that all jarring and discord may be prevented and love and peace after my decease [be] continued.[4]

Robert's descendants, and all those who have read over the years of his many trials during his sojourn on this earth, surely wish he himself likewise had finally found peace.

Notes

1   *Parish Register of St Mary Magdalene, Great Hampden, 1557–1812* Ed. by E. A. Ebblewhite (Aylesbury, Buckinghamshire, 1888), p. 78.

2   *Parish Register of St Mary's, Barnes, Surrey, 1538–1940.*

3   J. Whale, *One Church, One Lord* (London: SCM Press Ltd., 1979), p. 4.

4   Will of the Reverend Robert Lenthall, F. Farnsworth Starr, *The Eells Family of Dorchester, Massachusetts, 1633–1821* (Middle-town, Connecticut: 1903), pp. 188–190.

15

THE RISE OF
WILLIAM LENTHALL

ILLIAM LENTHALL, SECOND cousin to Robert, and nephew of St Robert Southwell, was born in 1591 at Henley-on-Thames. Born during his uncle's last fugitive year before his capture, and with these events as the background of his early family life, it would be surprising if William had not been raised Catholic. We see from his grandfather William's last will and testament, dated 1586, that he himself certainly had been. His father, also named William, had been born in 1525 at Latchford, Oxfordshire, and his mother was Frances Southwell, sister of Robert.

William also left St Albans Hall at Oxford University in 1609 without taking a degree, another sign that he may still have been a believing Catholic because all Oxford and Cambridge graduates were now compelled to recite an anti-Catholic oath in order to receive their degrees, and most Catholics refused to take the oath. Beginning in 1559, all graduates, judges and ministers throughout Elizabeth's entire realm had been forced to recite this 'Oath of Supremacy' which stated that the Queen was the supreme governor of the church. Catholics and some others refused to take the pledge, which ensured they were unable to run for Parliament. The oath was not rescinded until 1829 as part of the Catholic Relief Act.

Lenthall nevertheless was called to the bar at Lincoln's Inn in 1616 and by 1640 he represented Woodstock in the Short and Long Parliaments. He was never the popular, easygoing MP that his friend Hampden was—by all accounts he had difficulty persuading people to his line of thought—yet he was malleable, and that characteristic could be used to great effect.

Clarendon is very dismissive of Lenthall's suitability for the position of Speaker due to his 'timid' personality, mentioning only upon his selection that he was 'a lawyer of no eminent account.'[1] He continues, '(N)ot knowing how to preserve his own dignity, or to restrain the license and exorbitance of others, his weakness contributed as much to the growing mischief as the malice of the principal contrivers.'[2]

Still, when King Charles entered the House to seize the five members, violating the ancient privilege of that chamber, Lenthall had his finest hour, and when war began he was solidly in the Parliamentarian camp; that had not changed by the time of his friend Hampden's death. Lenthall carried on as Speaker after that watershed event, though he must have been disheartened by the sudden loss of his old family friend and classmate so soon after the great confrontation with King Charles in the House of Commons.

By June of 1644 the North was still solidly in the Royalists' grasp. The Marquis of Newcastle was besieged in York between the Scots and the Parliamentarians, but the Royalists under Prince Rupert were able to relieve the city and secure it as the Puritans withdrew westward until they reached Marston Moor. On 2 July the battle for the North ensued, with 27,000 troops and horse for the Puritans and only 11,000 foot and 7,000 horse for the combined Prince's and

Marquis' army.[3] In the end, the North was lost for Charles that day, with a total of 4,000 sons of England losing their lives on Marston Moor.

Pencil sketch of Great Haseley,
Oxfordshire Family History Centre and
PCC St Peter, Great Haseley.
Unknown artist

The last large, open-field clash of the Civil Wars took place at Naseby on 14 June 1645 between a Royalist force of half the number of the men under Fairfax and Oliver Cromwell. The Cavaliers tasted defeat again and Cromwell then became the undisputed master of the field.

William Lenthall, Speaker of the House of Commons
1640—1660
National Portrait Gallery

But according to Hyde, the basic question of the legality of the rebellion's leadership of the country still loomed as an issue for much of the populace. What right did Parliament truly have to overthrow the King and to rule in his stead? Could this military power truly develop the legal authority to rule over a country in peacetime? Once the Parliamentarian forces had triumphed, unease began to grow over these most fundamental of questions, and there was a growing fear of Parliament making laws completely unfettered by any other power.[4]

After the breakdown of negotiations between the King and the army, and the subsequent Engagement signed by Charles and the Scots, the Second Civil War began, pitting Cromwell's New Model Army against all other sectors of society—the Royalists, the established Church, the Scots, (as the King attempted to use his former foes to his advantage) and Parliament itself. Despite incredible odds, the Army triumphed. But according to Churchill,

> (I)t was the triumph of some twenty thousand resolute, disciplined military fanatics over all that England has ever willed or wished ... Thus the struggle, in which we have so much sympathy and part, begun to bring about a constitutional and limited monarchy, had led only to the autocracy of the sword.[5]

Lenthall continued as Speaker of the weakened body of the House of Commons until July 1647, when a mob comprising a cross-section of London's working class suddenly entered St Stephen's Chapel. Now having switched loyalties and unreservedly backing the Crown, they forced the members to repeal a law which would have re-established a Parliamentary militia. The

House of Commons, once the setting of Lenthall's finest hour—and indeed perhaps Parliament's finest hour, as its Speaker defended its members against a King acting like a despot—now saw the Speaker held down in his chair, just as Finch had been before him, and forced to invite the King back to London. Lenthall decided make a tactical retreat, fleeing for his protection to the relative safety of the Army.

London was now in a state of near chaos and Southwark, fearing anarchy, decided on its own to ask the Army to defend it. The borough gave free passage to the Parliamentarian forces, 18,000 strong, which then marched freely through the gates and over the Thames to Westminster and returned the Speaker to his chair.

Restored to his dignity, Lenthall continued doggedly in his position for the next two years, wrestling with a Parliamentary faction under the thumb of the 'Army Council' which had became the force behind all legislation. Denzil Holles, Hampden's old friend and comrade, was moved enough by this sad state of Parliamentarian affairs to write: 'The Army now did all, the Parliament was but a Cypher, only cry'd Amen to what the Councils of War had determined. They make themselves an absolute Third Estate.'[6]

Yet the Speaker had in his heart of hearts a partiality for the royal family, stating later after the Restoration that throughout the war he had sent funds to the King at Oxford and provided the Queen and their children with necessaries.

Beginning in 1647 the General Council of the Army drew up the first of what became a series of proposed new Constitutions which they thought fit to put before the Parliament. Influenced by the Levellers movement, and building on the ideas contained in the Petition of

Right of 1628, this 'Agreement of the People' called for universal male suffrage, electoral reform, the calling of a parliament every two years, and, for the first time in English history, religious freedom—except for the Catholics of the realm. Debated several times throughout the land, the articles contained in the various versions of the Agreement were eventually scrapped as no new Constitution was able to make its way toward a vote. Yet these ideas clearly remained in the public imagination and it is not difficult to discern the ultimate fruition of them in the articles of the Constitution of the United States.

Notes

1   E. Hyde, Earl of Clarendon, *History of the Rebellion and Civil Wars in England, Ed. By W. D. Macray* (Oxford: 1888), p. 44.
2   *Ibid.*, p. iii.
3   W. L. Churchill, *The History of the English-Speaking Peoples, Arranged for One Volume by Henry Steele Commager* (New York: Dodd, Mead & Co., 1956), p. 188.
4   Hyde, *History of the Rebellion*, p. xxii.
5   Churchill, *The History of the English-Speaking Peoples*, p. 193.
6   A. Fraser, *Cromwell, The Lord Protector* (New York: Alfred A. Knopf, 1973), p. 208.

16

CONFESSIONS

ESPITE THESE DEVELOPMENTS, there was some movement of Parliamentarians toward possible negotiation with Charles, and even a rumoured deal between Argyll and Cromwell which would have entailed 'the keeping of the King always in prison, and so governing without him in both kingdoms'[1] Whether or not that would have been at all feasible, or if there had been a formal pact, the agreement was understood to have been made between Cromwell and the Scots. Regardless, the outcome of these talks was indecisive, and Cromwell was obligated to stay in the North for the next six months, far away from the machinations of London politics.

On 22 December Cromwell and Speaker Lenthall called for Bulstrode Whitelocke and Sir Thomas Widdington to make overtures to the Army with the intent to cast some oil on the waters and save the King's life; however, within several days it became clear that the Parliamentarian armed forces would have none of it, and as soon as four days afterward Cromwell made his fateful speech abandoning the King to the mercy of the representatives of the people.[2] Deflecting the responsibility for Charles' life back onto his Creator, the Lord Protector declared 'Since the Providence of God hath cast this upon us, I cannot but submit to Providence, though I am not yet provided to give you my advice.'[3]

For Parliamentarians who had a Jacobin-like mindset of the absolute power of the people, it was just a small logical and political leap for them to put forth the next resolution on 28 December: to put King Charles on trial. On 4 January 1649 the House of Commons finally made the seemingly irrevocable break with English history by resolving on the revolutionary principle (again, to be echoed in America just a little more than a century later) that 'the people are, under God, the original of all just power — the supreme power of this nation.'[4] This statement incidentally made the Speaker, as the first representative of the body representing the people, in a way the head of state of the land and Lenthall was appropriately fêted at a ceremony in London which was thought by onlookers at the time to be (ironically) 'quasi-regal.'[5]

Regardless of his prior not-so-secret assistance to the royal family, Lenthall was obligated to put the question of Charles' execution before the members of this Rump Parliament (so called because of the disdain the people felt for the members still left in that body), but it was clearly a duty from which he recoiled.

In his *Confessions* Lenthall writes,

> Even then, I hoped the very putting the question would have cleared him, because I believed there were four to one against it, but they deceived me also … I make this candid confession, that it was my own baseness, cowardice, and unworthy fear to submit my life and estate to the mercy of those men that murdered the king, that hurried me on against my own conscience to act with them; yet then I thought that I might do some good, and hinder some ill.[6]

Despite the rather pathetic nature of this confession, one wonders what might have occurred had John Hampden been in Parliament to steer debate and perhaps even help Lenthall take more of a decisive stand against those who wanted to execute the King. After Colonel Thomas Pride's 'Purge' in December of 1648 which removed all those members of Parliament who did not support the execution, leaving possibly only half of the original members, there was little doubt about the outcome of any debate. Of course we have no way of knowing what course Hampden would have taken at this moral and political crossroads had he lived. But now being forced to work with men who would stoop to deceive the Speaker of the House by insinuating the question would be decided negatively, what chance did Lenthall have without his old friend to help and advise him?

At the time of his beheading, on 30 January in 1649, on a scaffold in front of the Banqueting House in Whitehall, Charles was allowed a moment to address the assembled masses. He expressed anguish over the execution of his great friend Strafford to which he had been forced to give his assent years earlier, truly believing that ultimately his own execution was God's retribution on him. He stated '(A)n unjust sentence that I suffered to take effect, is punished now by an unjust sentence on me'[7] and he expressed his hope that the ultimate peace of heaven would soon be his: 'I shall go from a corruptible to an incorruptible Crown, where no disturbance can be.'[8]

In making any attempt to give King Charles his due one must consider the well-known eulogy by his friend and adviser, the historian of the Rebellion, Lord Clarendon:

> He was the worthiest gentleman, the best master,
> the best friend, the best husband, the best father,
> and the best Christian that the age in which he
> lived had produced. And if he was not the best
> King, if he was without some parts and qualities
> which have made some kings great and happy,
> no other prince was ever unhappy who was
> possessed of half his virtues and endowments,
> and so much without any kind of vice.[9]

As Speaker of the House of Commons, William
Lenthall's name was not included on the death warrant
with the 59 regicide 'Commissioners' who had judged
Charles at the trial, a fact which in part allowed him
to escape the ultimate penalty upon Restoration. And
Lenthall was able to avoid the ignominy of having his
body disinterred later and thrown into an unmarked
mass grave, as the corpses of Pym and twenty other
Parliamentarians were in 1660. How much relief
William must have felt at that time, knowing that the
body of his old friend and classmate John Hampden
had been well secreted by his cousin Robert, never to
be exhumed for a public spectacle—and the private
humiliation of the family.

In August 1649, Cromwell turned his sights on
Ireland, to once and for all bring it (including what was
left of a Royalist/Catholic allied force there), to heel
under the sword of the Puritan power of England.
Surely the thousands who were to be killed by his
troops, and the many more thousands later to be
destroyed by his genocidal policies bore out the judgment of Hyde, who described Cromwell in one of his
most telling phrases as a 'brave bad man': 'In a word,
as he had all the wickedness against which damnation
is denounced and for which hell-fire is prepared, so he
had some virtues which have caused the memory of

some men in all ages to be celebrated and he will be looked upon by posterity as a brave bad man.'[10]

After Cromwell's return to England to face the threat of Charles II being declared King in Scotland, the Irish campaign was headed by his generals, including his son-in-law Henry Ireton. Until the 1653 surrender of the last Irish Catholic forces, the generals carried out a scorched-earth policy which attempted to destroy Catholicism and evict all Irish Catholics from their land. The practice of Catholicism was banned[11] and as many as 50,000 people were declared prisoners of war and deported to the Caribbean[12] while all Catholic-owned property was confiscated under the 1652 'Act for the Settlement of Ireland'. The total loss of life from all the battles of the Civil Wars was truly devastating — approximately 300,000 English people died in the Wars, amounting to a staggering six percent of the total population.[13] But the extent of the depredations in Ireland left a lasting impression for many years to come.

Churchill states

> Cromwell in Ireland, disposing of overwhelming strength and using it with merciless wickedness, debased the standards of human conduct and sensibly darkened the journey of mankind … Cromwell's record was a lasting bane. By an uncompleted process of terror, by an iniquitous land settlement, by the virtual proscription of the Catholic religion, by bloody deeds he cut new gulfs between the nations and the creeds. The consequences of Cromwell's rule in Ireland have distressed and at times distracted English politics down even to the present day. To heal them baffled the skill and loyalties of successive generations … upon all of us there still lies 'the curse of Cromwell.'[14]

One can only wonder how William Lenthall, nephew of a martyred Jesuit priest, reconciled this family history and, most likely, his own faith tradition, with the horrific and senseless slaughter that took place under Cromwell's direction. Could some of this history possibly have been changed if the Speaker had displayed sympathy for his fellow believers in Ireland and attempted to curtail Cromwell's depredations on that island?

As it was, history provided Lenthall with yet another humiliation to endure, and at the hands of Cromwell himself, when on 20 April 1653, the Rump Parliament was forcibly disbanded by the Lord Protector when he and thirty musketeers under the command of Major-General Thomas Harrison invaded the chamber and routed out the Speaker and the remnants of the members. The burning issue this time was whether or not this sitting of Parliament should completely dissolve and another slate of representatives be voted in; the MPs concern being that in the interim, there was no power in the realm that could assure any new elections would proceed lawfully. If the ultimate power of the state lay solely in the representatives of the people, how could any members feel confident that, without a sitting Parliament, there would be fair elections? However, if they could simply adjourn instead of dissolving, they could oversee the new elections. Cromwell, believing the MPs were loath to dissolve this sitting for fear they might never regain their seats, exploded in rage and marched from his offices in Whitehall to St Stephen's Chapel, shouting at his old friends and calling them variously 'whoremasters', 'drunkards' and 'corrupt and unjust'. When he came to Speaker Lenthall, Cromwell gestured at him and brutally called out 'Fetch him down.' Having no recourse, MP Thomas Harrison then literally pulled Lenthall off the Speaker's chair.[15]

Cromwell even ordered the troops to carry away the Speaker's Mace, the ancient symbol of Commons authority, and it was put into storage for years. The sight of drawn swords in the chamber, wielded at the behest of one who thought himself above the people, was understandably seen as a grave affront which insulted English tradition and history. Truly this was an action that in sheer contempt of the one institution which represented all English people knew no equal, including King Charles' 1642 'invasion' of the chamber; at least Charles forbore bringing armed men into St Stephen's Chapel.

These disturbing events led historian Antonia Fraser to remark

> One thing emerges from this whole extraordinary episode with incontrovertible clarity, and that is that Cromwell acted in a fit of uncontrollable passion, the kind of sudden berserk fury of which his career provides a number of bouts, including the famous massacre at Drogheda … His language alone in Parliament, the accusations of whoremastering, to say nothing of the physical manifestations of his rage such as the kicking of the very floor of the House of Commons, point to some deep-seated disturbance beyond ordinary frustration or mere exasperation.[16]

One can only speculate on what would have been the outcome had the situation been reversed and had Hampden been the survivor of the wars instead of his cousin Cromwell. Would the eloquent orator, adored by his friends and respected by his enemies, so skilled at reaching compromise, have ravaged Ireland, or been capable of bursting into St Stephen's Chapel with musketeers?

After the indignity of being dismissed in this brutal manner by Cromwell, Lenthall departed the political world for a time until he was elected Speaker of the First Protectorate Parliament. In the Second such Parliament, Lenthall strongly supported Cromwell's bid to be named King, but despite this he was not made Speaker and was not made a hereditary peer by Cromwell, as he had expected. Lenthall 'complained that he who had been for some years the first man of the nation, was now denied to be a member of either house of parliament; for he was incapable of sitting in the House of Commons by his place as Master of the Rolls, whereby he was obliged to sit as assistant in the other house.' Cromwell, aware of Lenthall's feelings, sent Lenthall a writ from his deathbed on 3 September 1658 which William believed was intended to grant him the hereditary peerage; upon receipt of which he was reportedly 'much elevated'.[17]

For this reason William declined the Speaker's position in the Commons at the Third Protectorate Parliament, called in May of 1659, until it was made clear to him that the body would not be assembled without his help. Lenthall then relented and accepted the Speakership, continuing on the seemingly never-ending rollercoaster ride that was his political career. Neither he nor his heirs would ever again be offered a peerage.

But the opening of Parliament in that year showed dramatically the divisions between officers of the army who had been responsible for calling the Parliament and certain other officers, namely Major-General Lambert and Lieutenant-General Fleetwood, who protested that Lenthall had been given too much power as the new, temporary Keeper of the Great Seal and as the one man who would be responsible for signing military and naval commissions instead of the commander-in-chief. In October of that year Lenthall's coach was stopped by Major-General Lambert as the Speaker was making his way to the chamber, and he was unable to open proceedings for two months.

Lenthall's fortunes again took a turn for the better in November, however, as General George Monck, commander-in-chief of the English army in Scotland, readied his men to confront Lambert and his soldiers as they marched north. Monck, realizing the instability of the country had reached a critical point, was ready to fight for the power of Parliament against the whims of the Army. But Lambert's men abandoned him before any confrontation could occur, and he returned to London with a bare remnant of his forces. Lieuten-ant-General Fleetwood, joined by forces loyal to Parliament, marched through the city on Christmas Eve 1659 and placed themselves at the Speaker's service in the street where he lived.

Lenthall appeared before them in his dressing gown as the officers made formal apologies to him, 'signifying their hearty sorrow for the great defection in this late interruption, with their absolute purpose of a firm adherence for the future; the like was done by the soldiers in their countenances and acclamations to the Speaker as they passed, owning him in words also as their general and the father of their country.'[18] To cap off the evening, Lenthall was escorted back to the Rolls house by soldiers holding torches. A new session of Parliament was now to be opened, with the Speaker in firm control once again, and as the country swung back politically from the precipice on which it had been teetering for the years of the Interregnum, Parliament would strive to restore unity to the fractured pieces of the realm.

Ever aware of the changing mood of the majority, William now understood that the English people as a whole had become tired of years of strife, and they desperately wanted a return of the monarchy as well as the stability and order it signified. Since the death of Cromwell in 1658, there had been a growing sense that the Protectorate's foundations were crumbling politically.[19] Likewise, General Monck, Cromwell's old Scottish commander, also had the political acuity to sense the changing times, and after Monck was invited by Parliament to return to London with his troops, he processed to the capital in 1660 like a conquering hero.

In Hyde's triumphant retelling of the events of May, the years of the Interregnum and Protectorate seemingly fell away magically upon the succession of the new sovereign:

> In this wonderful manner, and with this miraculous expedition, did God put an end in one month (for it was the first of May that the King's letter was delivered to the Parliament, and his Majesty was at Whitehall upon the 29th of the same month) to a rebellion that had raged near twenty years, and been carried on with all the horrid circumstances of parricide, murder and devastation, that fire and the sword, in the hands of the wickedest men in the world could be ministers of, almost to the desolation of two kingdoms, and the exceeding defacing and deforming the third. Yet did the merciful hand of God in one month bind up all these wounds, and even made the scars as indiscernible as in repeat of their deepness was possible.[20]

Notes

1   A. Fraser, *Cromwell, The Lord Protector* (New York: Alfred A. Knopf, 1973), p. 260.
2   *Ibid.*, p. 273.
3   *Ibid.*, p. 275.
4   W. L. Churchill, *History of the English-Speaking Peoples, Arranged for One Volume by Henry Steele Commager* (New York: Dodd, Mead & Co., 1956), p. 196.
5   *Commons' Journals*, vi, p. 226.
6   *Dictionary of National Biography/Confessions*, Old Parliamentary History, vol XXIII, p. 371.
7   C. Carlton, *Charles I: The Personal Monarch* (Second Edition) (London: Routledge, 1995), p. 353.
8   *Ibid.*, p. 354.
9   E. Hyde, Earl of Clarendon, *History of the Rebellion and Civil Wars in England, Ed. By W. D. Macray* (Oxford, 1888), p. 336.
10 *Ibid.*, p. xxvi.
11 J. Kenyon and J. Ohlmeyer, eds., *The Civil Wars: A Military History of England, Scotland and Ireland 1638–1660* (Oxford University Press: 2000), p. 141.
12 S. O'Callaghan, *To Hell or Barbados: The Ethnic Cleansing of Ireland* (New York: The O'Brien Press, 2013), p. 86.
13 Carlton, *Charles I: The Personal Monarch*, p. 304.
14 Churchill, *History of the English-Speaking Peoples*, p. 197.
15 Fraser, *Cromwell, Lord Protector*, p. 420.
16 *Ibid.*, p. 422.
17 E. Ludlow, *Memoirs of Edmund Ludlow, Esq. Lieutenant General of the Horse, Commander in Chief of the forces in Ireland, 1698–99* (Vevay, Switzerland: 1698), p. 596.
18 *Mercurius Politicus*, 22–9, December 1659.
19 P. Seaward, Preface to E. Hyde, Earl of Clarendon *The History of the Rebellion and Civil Wars in England, Ed. By W. D. Macray* (Oxford, 1888), p. xii.
20 Hyde, *History of the Rebellion*, p. 424.

17

VERMIS SUM

HE RETURN OF the monarchy in the person of Charles II truly marked a new era of forgiveness, mercy and reconciliation for the entire Kingdom—but perhaps a special time of redemption for Lenthall, after an entire political career that consisted of political vacillation coupled with an unerring instinct for self-preservation at all costs. The age-old English tendency to compromise and find common ground, something in which Lenthall had some experience, flourished anew when Charles II ascended the throne. According to Churchill,

> This was not only the Restoration of the monarchy; it was the restoration of Parliament. Indeed it was the greatest hour in Parliamentary history. The House of Commons had broken the Crown in the field; it had at length mastered the terrible Army it had created for that purpose ... Above all, everyone now took it for granted that the Crown was the instrument of Parliament and the King the servant of his people ... though the doctrine of Divine Right again was proclaimed, that of Absolute Power had been abandoned. The Restoration achieved what Pym and Hampden had originally sought, and rejected the excesses into which they had been drawn by the stress of conflict and the crimes and follies of war and dictatorship. The victory of the Commons and Common Law was permanent.[1]

However, in practice, the reality was that the laws of the realm now were pieces of legislation enacted, in many cases recently, by Parliament; not necessarily originating from the unwritten Common Law which had been considered the law of the land before the upheavals of the Civil Wars and the subsequent sea change in who actually had the right to establish laws. Churchill further states:

> During the years without a King, and without the Royal Prerogative, the idea had emerged that an Act of Parliament was the final authority. Coke's claim that the fundamental law could not be overborne, even by Crown and Parliament together, and his dream of judges in a Supreme Court of Common Law had been extinguished in England forever. It survived in New England across the ocean, one day to emerge in an American revolution directed against both Parliament and Crown.[2]

But despite the triumph of the ultimate symbol of the people, and the near-impossible accomplishment of surviving the most prominent political position within it, on a personal level fate had more humiliation in store for Lenthall. The penultimate indignity of William's public life occurred as a result of the Indemnity and Oblivion Act, passed in 1660, in which twenty men including Lenthall were excepted from the general amnesty for their actions during what was now being delicately termed 'The Interregnum'. Lenthall's name was only removed from this list as a result of General Monck mercifully speaking out on his behalf in the House of Lords; but part of the bargain was that he be barred from public office for the remainder of his life.

William then agreed, in what became his last political act, to serve as a witness against Thomas Scot, a regicide who had spoken against the King in Commons years prior. Most likely as a result of this favor to the King, Lenthall was invited to present himself at Court, an event which unwittingly provided the last humiliation in a political life fraught with nothing but trouble. When Lenthall attempted to kiss Charles II's hand, he leaned awkwardly as he was kneeling and fell backward, causing general guffaws and peals of laughter to issue from the assembled Court. Unfortunately for William this seemed to be the ultimate symbol of a career that veered from obsequiousness to the Crown to partisan support for the Parliamentarian cause, whenever it suited his interests.

Lenthall withdrew into retirement after this episode. He passed away at his home, Burford Priory in Oxfordshire, on 9 November 1662 and was buried at St John the Baptist Church in Burford. His will was replete with regret and recognition of his shortcomings as a statesman. William, just like his cousin the Reverend Robert Lenthall, who died in 1658—and his grandfather whose will we have from 1587—stated he wanted 'no Pompe' at his funeral,

> acknowledging myself to be unworthy of the least outward regard in this world, and unworthy of any remembrance that hath been so great a sinner. And I do further charge and desire that no monument be made for me, but at the utmost a plain stone, with this superscription only, *'Vermis Sum'* (in Latin, 'I am a worm').[3]

This is beyond doubt the tragic echo of his uncle St Robert Southwell's description of himself at his trial, from Psalm 22:7: 'I am a worm and not a man, scorned by everyone, despised by the people.'

Apparently no one in the family could bear to have a stone inscribed for him with such wording; there is no inscription at all on the stone over his grave, which is in the north aisle of the church. Considering the extreme care taken by various members of the Lenthall family to not be honored in any way after death, it is little wonder that there are so few reminders of the family name in Oxfordshire today.

But was this inscription William's way of finally revealing his identity as a Catholic, reclaiming his conscience as a man who, despite possessing real power, did nothing to help his fellow Catholics in England or Ireland during the entirety of his career? In yet another example of the heartbreaking irony of English life since the break with Rome, Lenthall had lived his public life on one side of the looking glass, pretending he was nothing but a devout Protestant, and swaying with the Puritan winds when it was expedient. Yet at the very end, when it was no longer necessary to pretend, he permitted himself to slip through to the other side of the mirror and, near death, unite his name with the public ignominy of his uncle's demise. Robert Southwell may indeed have considered himself a worm compared with Jesus; just as surely William must have seen himself as a true worm next to the heroic example of his Jesuit uncle.

No one can ever know if Lenthall ever ceased to be Catholic in his heart; indeed, it was related by several art historians and antiquarians, including John Loveday, that in William and Elizabeth's family manor, Burford Priory, there was a well-known portrait of the family of St Thomas More (including his in-law children) painted by Rowland Lockey after a lost original by Hans Holbein.

Hardly a subject most Protestant Englishmen would have featured in their works of art at home, it is fascinating to imagine Lenthall going about his business of state, rendering much more unto Caesar than he truly had to, under the tender gaze of this brilliant and heroic saint. By the end of his life—so fittingly for Lenthall—the painting, so symbolic of the ideal of the power of the individual's conscience against the absolute power of the state, was seen to have deteriorated, the paint rippling and in places chipping away. The painting was sold by the family in the 1800s and hangs, restored, in the National Portrait Gallery in London today.

Notes

1   W. L. Churchill, *History of the English-Speaking Peoples, Arranged for One Volume by Henry Steele Commager* (New York, Dodd, Mead & Co., 1956), p. 206.

2   *Ibid.*, p. 206.

3   *Wills from Doctors Commons* (Camden Society: 1863), p. 111.

18

ENLIGHTENMENT AND TRIUMPH

 OR ALL THE tragedy of St Robert Southwell's life of thirty-three years, we must realize he fulfilled what he undoubtedly saw as his mission on Earth to serve as a witness to the truth and to be an example of a man living out the dictates of his conscience. He enjoyed his fellowship with his Jesuit brothers and all the recusants who sheltered him at their great peril for the years he was on the run. He had as well the great blessings of knowing some of his writings such as *The Epistle of Comfort* were valued and appreciated during his lifetime and served to inspire others also undergoing persecution.

Reading his cousin William Shakespeare's *Venus and Adonis, The Rape of Lucrece, King Lear* and many of his other works, it is clear to see that Shakespeare did indeed, according to Southwell's dearest wishes, 'suit verse and virtue together', using many allusions to the current dire repression of society to pour out his anguish over what was happening in the only way he saw fit; with subtlety, and for those who had eyes to see it.

Perhaps another blessing in a very small but meaningful way was that at least Robert died in his own country. For he died at home, on English soil, unlike many English Catholics who were forced to live in exile during these years. Many of these people died abroad, never to return to their beloved country.

Joseph Pearce relates the story of one such man, Robert Peckham, who was buried in the church of San Gregorio in Rome, having died in 1564. His epitaph reads:

> Here lies Robert Peckham, Englishman and Catholic, who, after England's break with the Church, left England, not being able to live without the Faith, and who, coming to Rome, died, not being able to live without his country.[1]

Still, perhaps it mattered little where Southwell physically resided or where he died considering the celestial realm he inhabited spiritually. When in the poem *Content and Rich* we read the evocative phrase, 'My mind to me an empire is' we understand he never could be psychologically defeated regardless of any cruelty or torments he underwent in his last years on earth. More importantly, just as he knew that the pendulum would swing away from repression and toward freedom of religion and of thought, I feel he knew his country would eventually overcome the years of darkness and intolerance and would live up to the promise of the society which produced the Magna Carta, would eventually adopt the English Bill of Rights, and which would govern by the rule of law.

The Reverend Robert Lenthall likewise stayed his chosen course throughout his life, seemingly never despairing despite his humiliating disappointment in the American colonies and the unspeakable tragedy of losing most of his family after their return to England. Having learned lessons in humility the hard way, after he had tried to breathe 'the free aire of a New World'[2] Robert asked in his will that his burial be 'without Pompe'—the very phrase used by his great-uncle

William and his cousin William the Speaker in their wills. He humbly remained faithful to his God, returning to the Church of England, an institution he once had sailed across the Atlantic Ocean to avoid serving, putting aside his doctrinal issues with certain church practices while conforming to the realities of the day. Along with his cousin William, he made compromises to get along in the Carolingian world before true freedom of religion existed on their island.

William Lenthall had his finest hour when he spoke respectfully yet resolutely to his sovereign King Charles I, buying time for the five Parliamentary members as they escaped the House of Commons after Charles' invasion of the chamber. As the years went on, he became more interested in saving his own skin and remaining Speaker despite secretly helping the King and the royal family.

Although originally Catholic, he entered public life knowing he had to suppress his beliefs in order to hold office. Lenthall was in his own way a master of political compromise, something which doubtless enabled him to remain speaker for almost twenty years, a skill to be marveled at during times of almost unimaginable political tension and turmoil; but as we can see from his *Confessions*, the compromises he made with his own conscience finally caught up with him at the end of his life.

It is of course easy for all of us who live in the modern world of democratically-elected governments and constitutional monarchies to judge some of these men harshly and feel certain that, placed in similar circumstances today, we would always have the courage of our convictions.

Sadly, in the pre-modern world of the seventeenth century, with religious beliefs and political rights being threatened in every possible way, and draconian tortures and punishments awaiting those on the losing side, the instinct for self-preservation at all costs did win out at times.

Any evaluation of the life of John Hampden must conclude that he stayed true to his ideals of Puritanism and fought bravely for the right, as he saw it, to worship the way he desired, without the oppression of a state-run church or an absolute sovereign.

Although the Parliamentarians were responsible for several extreme excesses of zeal after they assumed power—during 'Pride's Purge' when duly elected pro-monarchist MPs were summarily expelled from Parliament; and when Cromwell, accompanied by armed troops, invaded the Rump Parliament and routed out all the members, taking possession of the Mace—the cause for which Hampden fought did make some progress in the realm of political and religious freedom. One of the acts passed by Parliament under Puritan control allowed Puritans to worship freely, and for the first time since Elizabethan days they were no longer forced to attend worship in the Anglican church.

Clarendon, as Lord Chancellor, later reversed this limited attempt at religious freedom by reinstating the Church of England as the state church in his 'Clarendon Code' despite Charles II's general disinterest in religion for its own sake. Charles perfectly mirrored the sentiments of his people in the spiritual realm, as the people of England now seemingly needed a release from the strictures of Puritanical Christianity. At one point during the years of the Commonwealth, adultery had actually been made a capital crime by the Parliamentarians. In his *History* Churchill observed 'the people of England did not wish to be the people of God in the sense of the Puritan God; they descended with thankfulness from the superhuman levels to which they had been painfully hoisted.'[3]

But the Rebellion did assure that England would not abide a system of absolute monarchy. Despite the language of the Magna Carta, and the traditional constitutional understanding that no English king was above the law, Charles had acted extralegally in imposing Ship Money; in invading the sanctity of the House of Commons in 1641; and perhaps in making alliances outside the country when his rule was threatened, trying to ensure that he would have ready forces to 'reduce' his country's rebels in case of attack. However, whether he deserved to be executed, especially when the House of Lords rejected a motion to try him for high treason, is another question entirely.

Cut down in the prime of life, as was Robert Southwell, Hampden showed complete dedication to his ideals and one wonders only how much more he would have contributed to the political progress of his country and the furthering of democratic ideals had he lived a normal span of years. Perhaps it would not have taken the passage of forty-five more years, with the accession of William of Orange in the Glorious Revolution of 1688, for Parliament to codify in the Bill of Rights the basic rights that all Englishmen should possess, while at the same time placing restrictions once for all on the royal succession and limiting many of the powers previously enjoyed by English monarchs.

The Bill of Rights was truly the culmination of centuries of strife and turmoil suffered by the English people, perhaps especially in the years of the Civil Wars, the deepest unrest the country had experienced — roughly the lifetimes of these four remarkable men. This legislation, a clear inspiration for the American act of the same name and the blueprint for civil order in the English-speaking world, was enacted in 1689.

In this act Parliament laid down a law stipulating there would be no taxation by the monarch (as the Ship Money tax had been) and that all new taxes must be approved by Parliament; there would be no standing army in peacetime (contrary to Charles I's actions when preparing for confrontation with the Parliamentarians) without Parliamentary approval; there would be complete freedom of speech within the Houses of Parliament and there would be no questioning of members' opinions stated in the chambers in a court of law, contrary to what had happened to Hampden as he stood trial for speaking out against Ship Money. Perhaps most meaningful of all, there could never again be 'cruel and unusual' punishment imposed by the state upon individuals — a standard of civilization without which many had suffered in the past, including in the early days of the New England colonies, and which came to be a cornerstone of American jurisprudence.

Still, even after all the years of strife and upheaval of the Civil Wars there were sadly many more years of darkness in the realm until the passage of the Bill of Rights. Several repressive pieces of legislation were passed, including the imposition of the various Acts of Uniformity which established the Book of Common Prayer and its rites as the only religious texts and practices allowed in the realm; the penal laws instituted in earnest in the reign of Charles II which banned municipal officials from belonging to any kind of nonconformist church; and the Test Acts, which prohibited all nonconformists from holding any public office whatever.

Moreover, Catholics had continued to pay exorbitant recusant fines to the Crown over the years. In the year 1612 alone records show the enormous sum of £371,060 received from the faithful.[4] The year 1664 saw the passage of the Conventicle Act wherein all churches and cathedrals in the realm finally and irrevocably became the property of the Church of England. Yet even after this, when it was apparent that English Catholicism as an entity was more or less vanquished, Catholics were still far from acceptance, or even tolerance, by the majority.

During the reign of Charles II there was widespread fear throughout much of society when the succession of James, the Duke of York, the brother of the King and a Catholic convert, loomed as a constitutional certainty. Possibly the only thing the public feared more than having a Catholic monarch, however, was rewarding illegitimacy by accepting James, Duke of Monmouth, Charles II's son by his mistress Lucy Walter, as King. Doing so would have controverted all that the institution of the monarchy stood for and would have set a frightening precedent of Parliament once again picking and choosing, and possibly deposing, the reigning monarch. Such chaos was so loathsome to the people as a whole that the 'Exclusion Bill' calling for the barring of the Duke of York from the throne was defeated in Parliament, and the Duke of Monmouth succeeded his brother to reign over a country deeply suspicious of his religious identity.

James II's reign was not marked, however, by a peaceful flourishing of religious freedom under the benign rule of the legitimate successor to the throne, which many Catholics and other nonconformists may have yearned for. His continued favoring of Catholics when appointing Army generals was noticed by all, and the explosion in the size of the standing army during his reign was of enormous concern to many, not just the Protestants of the realm.[5]

At the same time, in 1686, James suddenly decreed the stripping of many Protestant men of their arms through the implementation of the Militia Act, and the re-strengthening of the Game Act. Weapons these men had had the freedom to bear since ancient times according to their state in life were no longer legal. Governmental restrictions on arms were not new; Catholics had been banned from having certain arms for many decades but were allowed some weapons for self-defense. This was a more general disarming of a much greater part of the populace, however, and was justifiably seen as a sudden and alarming increase of royal power.

Additionally there was evidence that King James intended to suspend the Act of Habeas Corpus, which had been passed during the reign of his brother. Arguably England's single greatest contribution to the world of jurisprudence, the act stated that no man in the realm, regardless of social standing, could be imprisoned more than a few days without the existence of a reasonable body of evidence against him which must be provable in a court of law. This legislation codified a respect for the dignity of man and the power of any individual to resist the tyranny of the state—ideas which would spread throughout the entire English-speaking world along with the growth of the British Empire.

It began to be increasingly clear that the King now intended to re-establish Catholicism as a force in the country if not as the official religion of the land, imposing acceptance of the denomination, if need be, at the point of a gun. Not surprisingly King James faced such opposition that England was again facing the possibility of complete, open civil war; but peace was achieved and the realm brought back from the brink by James' escape and exile. After this so-called Glorious Revolution of 1688, years of warfare ensued between the new King, William, when James, allied with Louis XIV, attempted unsuccessfully to reestablish himself as monarch.

England was never to have another Catholic monarch, a ban which was codified in the Bill of Rights of 1689, passed after James' abdication—a stipulation which obviously curbed religious freedom but, seen through a different lens, allowed England to breathe freer, without feeling the constant threat of the religious pendulum swinging back yet again. And ironically, perhaps this feeling of freedom, over time, came to mitigate the defensive mindset of the people of England, and encouraged the softening of the harsh anti-Catholic statutes which had been the law of the realm for so many generations.

In 1778 came the passage of the so-called "Papists Act". For the first time in centuries Catholics in Great Britain and Ireland were recognized as having something approaching first-class citizenship by being allowed to own property again, and to inherit land. By 1782 Catholics were granted the ability to re-establish religious schools; by means of another act with perhaps greater import, in 1791 Catholic men were granted the vote as long as they owned property.

Finally, due to steadily-increasing pressure from public opinion, in 1829 Parliament passed the watershed 'Act of Catholic Emancipation', legislation which enabled British Catholics for the first time in centuries to enter the judiciary and the higher civil service, signifying a state of almost-complete legal equality with their fellow subjects. Property qualifications still excluded a good part of the populace, but this was nevertheless a watershed moment marking the end of the most draconian period of repression of Catholics in Great Britain. [6] (Just four years afterward, in 1833, slavery was abolished throughout the British Empire, thirty-two years before the United States would do the same).

Ensuring the dignity of every human being and guaranteeing his freedom of religion through the rule of law had gradually brought England out of the years of absolutism and repression into the Enlightenment and the modern age.

In the end, seen in a forgiving light, all the sacrifices, triumphs, and even the failings of these four men — all the experiences of the Great Rebellion in the years leading up to the Restoration, and of the turbulent years afterward — eventually became part of the fabric of the England that flourished under a strictly constitutional monarchy; the England that, from the later eighteenth century onward, became a symbol of freedom and respect for the rule of law and a political model for the rest of the entire world.

Notes

1 J. Pearce, *The Quest for Shakespeare* (San Francisco: Ignatius Press, 2008), p. 70.
2 S. E. Morison, *Builders of the Bay Colony* (Whitefish, Montana: Kessinger Publishing), p. 40.
3 W. L. Churchill, *History of the English-Speaking Peoples, Arranged for One Volume by Henry Steele Commager* (New York: Dodd, Mead & Co., 1956), p. 208.
4 Pearce, *Quest for Shakespeare*, p. 152.
5 Churchill, *History of the English-Speaking Peoples*, p. 220.
6 *The History of Parliament Trust* as part of *British History Online http://www.british-history.ac.uk/commons-jrnl/vol8*

APPENDIX

An Oxfordshire Recusant's Pick and Mix Will

Anthony Hadland

The following article was first published in *The Journal of the Oxfordshire Family History Society*, Volume 27 N° 2 (August 2013). In this article, 16th century spellings have been modernized.

 N February 1587, the year before the Spanish Armada, William Lenthall of Latchford, Great Haseley, Oxfordshire, made his will. He died later in the year and probate was granted that November.

The Lenthalls came to Oxfordshire from Herefordshire in the 15th century. William Lenthall was the grandson of Sir William Lenthall and the son of Thomas Lenthall, both of Latchford, Great Haseley. Both grandfather and father were buried in the family vault at Great Haseley parish church, as indeed was William himself, as his will directed.

Bonds of kindred and marriage connected William Lenthall to many recusant Catholic families. His great aunt Margaret Lenthall married Robert Tempest of Holmside, Co. Durham and via that connection William was related to the Moores of Oxfordshire and the Belsons. Eighteen years before William Lenthall wrote his will, the Tempests had been involved in the Rising of the North, which had triggered the Pope's excommunication of Elizabeth I, and two years after William's death, young Thomas Belson was martyred at Oxford in the crackdown after the Armada.

William himself married Jane Brome from the nearby Boarstall, Buckinghamshire, recusant family. Their daughter Elinor married into the recusant Horseman family of Great Haseley, famous for the clandestine burial of Elizabeth Horseman in Holton parish church some 40 years after William Lenthall's death.

A son of William and Jane, another William Lenthall, married Frances Southwell, sister of the Jesuit poet and martyr Robert Southwell. Their son William, born in Henley-on-Thames in 1591, matriculated at St Alban's Hall, Oxford, but did not receive a degree. This would be typical of a recusant Catholic student, who could study at university but could not in good conscience take the anti-Catholic oath required formally to graduate. However, any attachment he had to Catholicism was soon abandoned. He became a lawyer and subsequently Speaker of Parliament for much of the period from the latter years of the reign of Charles I through the Civil Wars and Protectorate until the Restoration of the monarchy. His remarkable survival was only achieved by bending, like the mythical Vicar of Bray, whichever way the wind blew.

Speaker Lenthall wrote his own Latin epitaph, acknowledging his lack of principle: *Vermis sum*, which translates as 'I am a worm'. Following the example of his grandfather, the subject of this article, he specified that he should be buried 'without pomp'. Speaker Lenthall having purchased Burford Priory in 1637, it had by this time become the main residence of the Lenthall family. They conformed to the Church of England and Lenthall was therefore interred in Burford parish church.

Returning to the matter of the burial of the Speaker's grandfather, William Lenthall of Latchford, he chose to be buried in the family vault at the parish church of St Peter, Great Haseley. This was quite normal for a recusant gentry family and was certainly not, of itself, an indication of conformity to the Church of England: it was the family vault, in the local church, built by Catholics for Catholic worship. The fact that the Church of England was not currently in communion with Rome was not going to stop recusant gentry from using their family chapels or vaults. In any case, recusants hoped it might not be long before union with Rome was resumed. To this day there are gentry families who have always been Roman Catholic yet who have aisles, chapels or vaults in parish churches which became Anglican at the Reformation. An Oxfordshire example is the Blount (now Eyston) family aisle at Mapledurham parish church.

What was much more remarkable was that William Lenthall left money from former chantry lands, bought from the Crown, to pay for the *'de profundis'* psalm, to be said by four poor men of the parish kneeling before his grave. The *'de profundis'* had been stripped from the Anglican liturgy in the 1552 Book of Common Prayer and prayers for the dead were the antithesis of Protestantism.

It is this *'de profundis'* psalm, as quoted in Lenthall's will, that in early 2013 caught the attention of the coordinator of the Oxfordshire Family History Society's programme of transcription of Oxfordshire wills, who wrote to ask my opinion of the wording. He was aware of the uncertain situation concerning the Catholic church's approval of English translations of Biblical texts during this period. As William Lenthall was a recusant Catholic, which English translation of the psalm did he quote in his will?

We know that William Lenthall was still a recusant at the end of his life because, in 1586, the year before he wrote his will and died, he was on a list of Oxfordshire Catholics who compounded for unpaid recusancy fines. (In this context, 'compounding' means submitting a bid to the Crown to pay a discounted lump sum to clear their debts.) He and his wife and daughters headed the list, offering £20; his son proffered a mere £2.

Yet at first glance, William's will could be mistaken for a Protestant one. It includes the prayer:

> Almighty God with whom do live the spirits of them which do depart here in the Lord and in whom the souls of them that be elected after they be delivered from the burden of the flesh be in joy and felicity...

This is plainly based on a prayer in the order of burial in the *Book of Common Prayer*. Here is the *BCP* version, which is virtually the same apart from the absence of punctuation in Lenthall's version:

> Almighty God, with whom do live the spirits of them that depart hence in the Lord, and in whom the souls of them that be elected, after they be delivered from the burden of the flesh, be in joy and felicity...

But later in the prayer, we find that he has changed the wording from 'all other departed in the true faith of thy holy name' to 'all others departed in the true faith of the holy Catholic Church'. Although the Church of England considered itself still to be the Catholic church in England (but now independent of Rome), this form of words does not appear in this prayer in any contemporary edition of the *Book of Common Prayer* that the writer has been able to trace. So it seems Lenthall was making a point regarding his recusancy, albeit in a muted way.

Also, the very fact that the will specifies that four poor men of the parish should recite the *'de profundis'* psalm at his grave 'yearly for ever upon Sundays and festival Days within my said Chapel' within Great Haseley parish church is highly suggestive of traditional Catholicism. As a reward for their prayers, these four poor men were to receive every year a frieze coat (that is, one made of heavy, coarse, woollen material) funded from the income from 'Concealed Lands' purchased by William Lenthall from the Queen. In effect, Lenthall was attempting to maintain the pre-Reformation Catholic practice of a chantry chapel within what had become a Protestant church. It should be remembered that the whole business of prayers for the dead (many of whom were presumed by Catholic theology to be in Purgatory, having their past sins purged whilst awaiting admittance to Heaven) was a key issue of the Reformation and was rejected by Protestants. For example, Article 22 of the Church of England's 39 Articles, states:

The Romish Doctrine concerning Purgatory… is a fond thing, vainly invented, and grounded upon no warranty of Scripture, but rather repugnant to the Word of God.

Yet here was William Lenthall trying to set up a chantry chapel in the parish church, 42 years after Henry VIII's Chantries Act, 40 years after that of Edward VI and 28 years after Elizabeth I's Act of Uniformity, all of which were intended to sweep away such things.

And then we come to the question of which translation of the '*de profundis*' does William Lenthall quote.
(Confusingly, this psalm may be referred to either as
number 129 or 130. It is number 130 in the Hebrew
numbering adopted by the Protestant reformers,
whereas it is 129 in the Greek numbering traditionally
used by the Roman Catholic and the Orthodox
churches. Modern Catholic translations, however, use
the Hebrew numbering.)

William Lenthall's will shows him, in all respects,
to be a micro-manager on a grand and almost neurotic
scale. He even splits the psalm up, specifying which
of the four poor men should recite which sentence. But,
stripping out these instructions, this is the translation
William Lenthall gives:

> Out of the depth have I called unto the Lord:
> Lord hear my voice, for there is mercy with thee.
> I look for the Lord,
> my soul doth wait for him,
> in his word is all my trust.
> If thou O Lord wilt narrowly mark what is done amiss,
> O Lord who may abide it?
> O Israel trust in the Lord,
> for with the Lord there is mercy,
> and with him is plenteous redemption.
> And he shall redeem Israel from all his sins.

At the time the will was written, English Roman
Catholics already had an English translation of the
New Testament, officially approved by the Vatican.
This was published at Reims, France, in 1582. It is
highly probable that William Lenthall had access to
one of the many copies smuggled into England. But
the companion Old Testament, containing the psalms,
was not published in complete form until 23 years after

Lenthall's death. That was at Douai, now in France but then in the Spanish Netherlands, in the year 1610. Hence the first Vatican-approved standard English translation Roman Catholic Bible was known as the *Douai-Rheims* or *Rheims-Douai* version. Douai, a Flemish town, was variously spelled by English Catholics as Douay or Doway. The first syllable rhymed with 'cow', reflecting the Flemish pronunciation, rather than French.

The nearest thing to a Vatican-approved English translation of the '*de profundis*' psalm available to William Lenthall was that in the Marian primer ('Marian' here meaning 'of the reign of Queen Mary I'). This was published during Mary Tudor's short and tragic reign, under the approval of Cardinal Reginald Pole. Contrary to what some believe, Mary's regime was an enthusiastic user of the printing press. The Marian primer, officially entitled *An Uniform and Catholyke Prymer in Latin and Englishe*, was reprinted 34 times — an average of roughly every six weeks during Mary's reign. Here, taken from the Dirige or burial service, is its version of the psalm:

> From the deep places have I called unto thee:
> (O Lord) Lord hear my voice.
> Let thine ears be intentive, to the voice of my prayer.
> If thou (Lord) wilt look too straightly upon sins:
> O Lord, who shall abide it.
> But there is mercy with thee:
> and because of thy law, have I abiden thee, O Lord.
> My soul hath abiden in his word:
> my soul hath trusted in our Lord.
> From the morning watch unto night:
> let Israel trust in our Lord.
> For with our Lord there is mercy:
> and his redemption is plenteous.

And he shall redeem Israel: from all the iniquities of it.

This differs in a number of ways from Lenthall's version. Interestingly, his 'Out of the depth' anticipates the much later 1611 Authorized Version's 'Out of the depths'. The reformer Miles Coverdale's 1535 version of the psalm, the basis of the versions used in various editions of the *Book of Common Prayer* and in the Elizabethan *Bishops' Bible*, has 'Out of the deep'.

Also, Lenthall's 'If thou O Lord wilt narrowly mark what is done amiss, O Lord who may abide it?' seems to be a hybrid of the Protestant Thomas Becon's 'for if thou shouldest narrowly mark our iniquities, O Lord, who shall abide it?' (in *The Flower of Godly Prayers*) and Miles Coverdale's version, which has, 'If thou, Lord, wilt be extreme to mark what is done amiss, O Lord, who may abide it?'

It is intriguing to see Lenthall's 'pick and mix' approach to the religious elements of his will. As the poet and former recusant Catholic turned Anglican clergyman John Donne put it 37 years later,

'No man is an island, entire of itself; every man is a piece of the Continent, a part of the main'. We can see, in William Lenthall's will of 1587, evidence of his attempts to combine loyalty to the marooned religion of his forefathers with the religious practice of the community at large in the parish church of those very same ancestors.

The Will of William Lenthall

Author's note

HE FOLLOWING WILL— what I once thought of as a will only a descendant could love—is included in part because wills are an invaluable genealogical and historical resource and I thought it necessary for reference with Mr Hadland's article. But I came to appreciate it more as time went on, for several reasons.

I thought the obvious extreme (some might say obsessive) attention to detail was a bit humorous at first—but I gradually realized a possible meaning for the unending legalisms and repetition. If one's livelihood, family reputation and indeed one's very own life were constantly threatened by one's own country, *and its legal system had been already used against your family to destroy your fortune and possessions,* would one not take extraordinary care to dictate exactly where your resources should be directed? William takes the greatest possible pains to distribute exactly what he intends each and every family member and friend to receive, making sure nothing will go to the state if at all humanly possible.

Another interesting aspect of the will is in the section dealing with Isabell, William's second wife. As is well known, the laws of primogeniture in England made it impossible for women to inherit real estate unless they were the sole offspring of their parents. In this document William goes to incredible lengths to ensure Isabell will want for none of her familiar creature comforts in her future life as his widow.

Although females could not inherit the actual manor house, they could inherit every single object in the house, and this is exactly what happened in this case, with the manor at Lachford. Edmonde is the heir to the manor at Lachford as well as all the contents of the manor—but it is Isabell who will inherit every single movable item, and some non-movable ones, such as the 'glasse windowes' and 'wainskotts' inside the manor at Latchford—and have all her things around her for the rest of her life. In those days forty pounds would have been enough to purchase a small, modest house, and presumably Isabell would have arranged all her familiar objects around her, to be a comfort in her older years.

Through the dense legalese of the will can be glimpsed a man who cared so deeply for his wife, to whom he had been married only a few years, that he would strip bare his manor to the very walls to ensure she would want for nothing.

Women play so little part in this family story as I have written it simply because I refused to invent personalities, conversations and situations that were not recorded at the time. But as a descendant of this family, it was reassuring that, for all the marginalization of women in the seventeenth century and for centuries to come, at least I know beyond a shadow of a doubt that this lady was loved and cherished by her husband.

The Will of William Lenthall, PROB 11/71

 N THE NAME of God Amen. I, William Lenthall the elder of Lachford in the County of Oxon Esqiuer, being at the present in good health of bodye and of perfect mind and Remembraunce I thanck Almighty God therefore Considering the uncertainty of this transitory Lyfe Doe this present fifteenth Daye of ffebruary in the nine and twentieth years of the Reigne of our Soveraigne Ladye Elizabeth by the grace of God England ffrance and Ireland Quene Defendor of the faithe etc.

And in the yeare of our Lorde God one thousand five hundredth and eighty and six make and ordayne this my Last will and testament in manner and form following that is to saye first I commit my sowle into the most holy and blessed protection and keeping of our savyo' and Redeemer Jesus Christ. And my body to be buried in the parrishe Churche of Saincte Peter and Paule in Greate Hastley within my Chappell there where my grandfather William Lenthall and my father Thomas Lenthall doe lye buryed over which place or grave I will that my executor hereunder named doe Laye within one yeare or two at the farthest next after my decease a plate of brass or Alibaster stone ____ in the Wall over my grandfathers monument thereon engraved the several times of our departures out of this World.

The ordering of my burial I referre to the discrec'on of my Executor. But my meaning is that it be donne without pompe. At which time of my burial I will there be distributed amongst the poorest of the townes next adjoining to Lachford forty shillings. And to the poorest householders inhabiting within the parrishe of great Haseley to every Couple twelve pence. And to some of the Couples twoe shillings at the discrec'on of my said Executor. Also I will that my said Executor doe give to four of the poorest men of the parish Haseley aforesaid each of them a frieze Coate to attend upon my funeral.

Also I will that such four frieze Coates shalbe given by my sonne William Lenthall his heirs or assignes for ever owte of his Concealed Lands which I purchased of the Quene in Stunsfield and Haseley aforesaid to four of the poorest men in the parrishe of Haseley yearely for ever uppon Sondayes and festival Dayes within my said Chappell ymediatly when service is done in token of profession of my faithe saye these words taken out of the holy scripture. Kneeling on their Knees:

> Owte of the Depthe have I called unto the Lord: Lord heare my voice, for there is mercy with the I Looke of the Lord, my sowle doth wayte for him, in his word is all my trust.

This to be said first by one of them. And the second thus:

> Yf thou Oh Lorde wilt narrowly marke what is donne amiss, Oh Lorde whoe maye abide it. Oh Israell Trust in the Lorde, for with the Lorde there is mercy, and with him is plenteous redemption. And he shall redeem Israell from all his sinnes.

And the third thus:

> I knowe that my Redeemer Liveth and that I shall rise out of the Earthe in the last Daye and shalbe covered againe with my skynne and shall see God with my flesh yea and my self shall behold him not with other but with these same eyes.

Which said all fower shall joyne in this prayer:

> Almightye God with whom doe live the spiritts of them whiche doe depart heare in the Lorde and in whom the sowles of them that be elected after they be delivered from the burden of the fleshe be in joye and felicity wee give the harty thancks for that it hathe pleased thee to deliver this our brother William Lenthall owte of the miseries of this sinnefull world beseeching that it maye please of thy gracious goodness shortly to accompte him in the number of thy Electe. And to hasten thy Kingdome that we with this our brother and all others departed in the fine faith of the holy Catholique Churche maye have our perfecte Consumac;on and bliss bothe of body and sowle in thy eternal and everlasting glory. Amen.

Also I will that my Executor shall give to my wife and daughters eache of them a blacke gowne. And to foure or more of my servantes at my funeral black Coates at the discrec'one of my Executor.

Item I give to Anne Lenthall my sonne John Lenthalls daughter the som'e of three score pounds of Lawfull Englishe money when the said Anne shall accomplish thage of Eightene years yf the saide Anne shall soe longe live.

Item I give to William Lenthall second sonne to my sonne John lenthall deceased the some of fifty powndes to be delivered unto him Lykewise at thage of Eightene years yf he Lykewise so longe shall live.

Item I give to William Tempest and Nicholas Piggott ffifty pounds to be bestowed in such manner and form and at such time as the said William Tempest and Nicholas Piggott my Loving and trusty friends together with my Executor at their discrec'ons shall thinck most fitt and convenient according to a special direction of my minde and pleasure which they onely know touching my Daughter Elynor.

And where I meant to give and bequeathe unto Edmond Lenthall my sonne John Lenthalls eldest sonne absolutely all that residue of the farme of Greate Haseley not already conveyed unto my sonne William Lenthall, and nowe am enforced the meaning of some to be hereafter to procure suters and controv'sies betwene the said Edmond and my said sonne for or concerning messuages, Landes, tenements or hereditaments called the Burroughe, Rem_____ and Stunsfield or some parte thereof already conveyed unto my said sonne William Lenthall of an estate of inheritance I doe nowe give and bequeathe unto the said Edmond Lenthall when he shall accomplish the age of three and twenty yeares yf he the said Edmonde so long shall live.

All the said Residue of the farme of Greate Haseley aforesaid for so many yeares as shall be then to come unexpired in my Lease made to John Oglethrope upon this condic'on that if the saide Edmond or his heires or assignes after he shall accomplish thage of one and twenty years shall not or doe not at any time uppon request made unto him by the saide William his heires or assignes sufficiently convey and assure release and extinguish at the Cost and Charge of the said William his heires Executors or assigned the aforesaid messuages, Lands, tenements and hereditaments and all his Righte, Title Interest and demand of in and to the same unto the said William his heirs and assigned may quietly enjoy the premises according to the Conveyance thereof already to him made by me the said William. Then this present gift and bequest abovesaide shall cease and be voide. Anything herein conteyned to the Contrary notwithstanding. And from thensforthe shall fully come remaine and be to my said sonne to his sole and proper use and behufe and to no other intent or purpose.

Also I will that my Executor hereunder named doe Distribute to other poor man at his discrec'on to be chosen and appointed owte for twoe yeares next after my burial tenne pounds a Yeare. Also I give to the Churchwardens of the parrishe Churche of Greate Haseley aforesaid towards the Reparac'ons of the same Churche forty shillings. Also I give to the poore prisoners in the Castell of Oxforde three shillings four pence. To the Prisoners of Wallingford Castell three shillings four pence. To the Prisoners of Ailesbury gaole three shillings four pence to be paide within one moneth after my decease.

Also I give to my brother Richard Lenthall such Apparrell as appeareth by the Schedule hereunto annexed. Also I give to Robert Lenthall his sonne one Cowe and Ten sheepe or five pounds in money for a stock towards his bringing up.

Also I give to Anne Horseman my Daughter Horsemans daughter tenne pounds to be paide and delivered unto her at her daye of marriage yf she so long shall live, so that she doe marry by the consent and good liking of my Executor and overseers or of the most parte of them whereof I will my executor to be one.

Also I give and bequeath to Isabell my nowe Wyfe forty pounds of good and lawful Englishe money in Liewe of a howse to have bene provided for her according to my Coven'nte touching the same conteyned in a pair of Indentures bearing the date the twentieth daie of Januarye in the fourth years of the Reigne of our Soveraigne Ladye the Quenes Maiestie that nowe is made between me on the one partye and Hugh Cartwrighte Esquier, John Wilkins, Martyn James and William Payne gent on thother partye.

And also albeyt I have made unto my Wyfe a great Joincture in Respecte of that small porc'on I had with her, Yet nevertheless for that I have found her a Loving Wyfe unto me and uppon the sure hope and confidence she will continue the like towards all my Children, therefore for the better supply of all such necessary houwsehold implements as shalbe necessary for her housekeeping in Lachford howse being parcel of her Joincture, I will therefore that my executor hereunder named shall permitt and suffer her to have and enjoye the use and occupying of all such howseholdstuffe and utensils as been conteyned in a Scedule hereunto annexed subscribed with the hand and seale of me the saide William Lenthall for and during her natural lyfe. So that she the said Isabell my Wyfe doe at such time as she shall require the Deliverye thereof at my Executors hands with twoe sufficient suretyes become sufficiently bound in the double value thereof.

With Condic'on or Condic'ons that the said sureties theire executors or Administrators shall within six Weeks next after her Decease safelye either redeliver all and singular the saide goods and Chattells in the saide Schedule conteynd or all such the value of every of the same and of every part thereof as shale conteynd and sett downe in the saide Inventarye unto my said Executor hereunder named at the Choice and election in part or in the wholle of my said Executor.

Also I doe further give and bequeath to my saide Loving wife to her owne use for ever all her Apparrell, one litle goulde Cheyne which she hath com'only used to weare, her brasseletts, Rings, Juells and Tabletts and one Casting bottell of silver Double gilte, twoe of my geldings or naggs, twoe paire of Corsletts with twoe pikes furnished for footemen and two Calivers with their murryons, flasks and touche boxes.

Item I give to the saide Edmond Lenthall as things to goe contynue and remaine allwayes to and with the heires and owners of my Mannor of Lachford suche goods and Chattells as appeareth by the schedule hereunto annexed to be given unto him All which parcells I will shalbe delivered unto him when he shall accomplishe thage of twenty and three yeares yf he so Longe shall live.

Item I give to William Lenthall my sonne as Legatorye and as my speciall bequest otherwise then in repecte of his executorship as things annexed to remaine with his howse Lands and ten'tes called the Boroughe such parcells of plate as within the schedule hereunto annexed dothe Lykewise appeare.

Item I give to every one of my Daughters that be maryed forty shillings apeece. And to either of theire husbands tenne shillings apeece as a token of Remembraunce.

Item I give to every of my sister Pigotts sonnes eache of them tenne shillings apeece.

Item I give the lyke to my twoe Cosens Robert and William Tempeste and the Lyke to theire sister my neece Belson.

Item I give to Robert and Constance Knightley his sister five poundes apeece to be delivered unto them when they attayne unto thage of one and twenty yeares yf they so Longe shall live.

Also I give to John Mayborowe my serv'nte six and twenty shillings eighte pence a yeare owte of my howse in Henlye so Longe time as my executor shall have estate and interest therein yf he my saide serv'nte doe so Longe live.

Also I will that my sonne William Lenthall shall yearely for ev' distribute amongest the poorest howse-holders in Haseley allwayes on Ashwednesdaye six shillings eighte pence owte of the concealed Lands which I purchased of the Quene in Haseley.

Also I give unto my sonne William Lenthall and to his heires if it be not already sufficiently conveyed all my saide Concealed Lands which I purchased of the Quene in Haseley and Stunsfield and Lykewise my Chauntery Lands there in Haseley.

Item I give to my Welbeloved frende John Boyer a golde Ringe in token of Remembraunce.

And finally my debts paid my ffuneralls and Lega-cies discharged all other my goods and chattells aswell reall as personal before not bequeathed nor given hereby I doe give and bequeathe to William Lenthall my sonne whome I make my full and sole Executor of this my Last will and testament.

Also I do ordayne and make my Welbeloved frende Robert Williams of Kymball Esquire my supervisor and overseer of this my Last will and testament.

And doe give him for his paines herein to be taken a peece of plate or forty shillings in money. In wittnes whereof I the saide William Lenthall to this my present Last will and testament have putt my seale of armes and countermaund all former Willes by me made the saide William Lenthall at any time heretofore made. And do openly pronounce and testifye this to be my Last will and testament. And none other Wittnes to this will conteyning three sheetes of paper and one sheete for the Scedule Nicholas Piggott Richard Piggott William Lenthall Junior.

A Scedule annexed of suche goods and Chattells as within this testament are bequeathed and Lefte herein to be expressed.

Inprimis to my Wyfe the use and occupying of all suche necessary howsehold stuff as are belonging to the Hall, Parlo'r, Buttrye, Chambers and in all other howses of office as hereafter followeth that is to saye in the Hall the Tables, formes, stooles thereunto belonging with the portalls, wainskott, glasse windowes for the Chimney, a fyre forke, a paire of Aundyrons, A paire of tongs in the Parlo'r. A Longe table with the frame for the stooles, formes and benches thereunto belonging. A folding table, twoe Chaires, A Cupbord, the portalls, glasse windowes and all wainskott aboute the Parlo'r. A paire of Aundyrons, a fire shovell and tongs sutable to the same for the Chimney. In the Buttrye the Bynnes for breade, the shelves, the table with tressells, Candlesticks, glasses and potts. The standers and hoggesheads for beare nowe being in use there in the Chamber. The furniture there as wainskotts, hangings, bedstedd and bedds furnished as they nowe are with Cupborde, Chaires and glass windowes. And Lykewise all other howses of Office furnished as they nowe be. Whiche stuffs my meaning is shalbe imployed onely in and uppon my saide howse in Lachford and not ells wheare, and be repayred and mayteyned from time to time.

Item I give to my brother Richard Lenthall my two best gownes, twoe cassocks, twoe payre of drawers and five markes in money.

Item I give to my serv'ntes (that is to saye) To John Hall to George ffrancis To William Hinton eache of them tenne shillings a peece. And to William Pilkington forty shillings. To Anne Carden my Chamber-maide six shillings eighte pence.

To Edmond Lenthall and theire males that shall please God to succede as heires to Lachford these utensils following (that is to saye): In the Parlour the Longe table with the frame, stooles and benches, the Courte Cupborde, a Chaire, wainskott and glasse windowes in the Chimney. Aundyrons, tongs, fire shovell and fyreforke. In the Hall twoe Long tables with the frame and formes and benches, wainskott and glasse windowes with twoe Chambers furnished with bedding and bedstedds with Cubbord and Chaires thereunto belonging. In the Buttrye the Binnes for breade, the shelves and standers for drinck. In the Kitchin the yron Racke, the barre of yron with two hangers for potts, in spitts twoe, in brasse potts twoe.

Item I give more to my Daughter Horseman a hunderd pounds owte of one of my Daughters por-tions. Yf any of them Dye before theire mariage whiche portions are not to be delivered unto them at all if they dye before they be maryed.

Item I give to everye of my godchildren five shil-lings apeece or a sheepe at the discrec'on of my Exec-utor.

Probatum fuit Testamentum suprascriptum apud London Coram Venerabili viro m'ro Will'mo Drury Legum Doctore Curie Prerogative Cant: Mag'ro Custode sive Com'issario etc Sexto Die Mensis Novem-bris Anno D'ni Mill'imo Quingentesimo Octo-gesimo Septimo Juramento Will'mi Lenthall filij naturalis et l'timi dicti defunt'executoris in hu'mo'i testamento nominat' Cui commissa fuit.....................

[*Proved at London (PCC) 6 Nov 1587 by the oath of William Lenthall the son and executor*]

INDEX

Lightning Source UK Ltd.
Milton Keynes UK
UKOW08f1928110517
300981UK00003B/92/P